NEXUS PSYCHOTHERAPY

NEXUS PSYCHOTHERAPY
Between Humanism and Behaviorism

By

KENNETH URIAL GUTSCH
Director, Program of Counseling Psychology
University of Southern Mississippi
Hattiesburg, Mississippi

and

JACOB VIRGIL RITENOUR, II
Chief Clinical Psychologist
Psychological Services Unit
State Prison of Southern Michigan
Jackson, Michigan

With a Foreword by

Howard S. Rosenblatt
Staff Psychologist, Appalachian Hall Hospital
Professor of Psychology
University of North Carolina at Asheville

and

Harold H. Dawley, Jr.
Staff Psychologist and Coordinator of Psychological Research
Veteran's Administration Hospital, New Orleans
Department of Psychiatry and Neurology
Tulane University School of Medicine

CHARLES C THOMAS · PUBLISHER
Springfield · Illinois · U.S.A.

Published and Distributed Throughout the World by
CHARLES C THOMAS • PUBLISHER
BANNERSTONE HOUSE
301-327 East Lawrence Avenue, Springfield, Illinois, U.S.A.

© *1978, by* CHARLES C THOMAS • PUBLISHER

ISBN 0-398-03734-5

Library of Congress Catalog Card Number: 77-12383

With THOMAS BOOKS *careful attention is given to all details of
manufacturing and design. It is the Publisher's desire to present
books that are satisfactory as to their physical qualities and artistic
possibilities and appropriate for their particular use.* THOMAS
BOOKS *will be true to those laws of quality that assure a good
name and good will.*

Printed in the United States of America
N-1

Library of Congress Cataloging in Publication Data

Gutsch, Kenneth Urial.
　Nexus psychotherapy.

　Bibliography: p.
　Includes index.
　1. Psychotherapy.　2. Humanistic psychology.　3. Behaviorism,　I.
Ritenour, Jacob Virgil, joint author.　II. Title.
RC480.5.G87　　　　　　　　　616.8'914　　　　　　　　　77-12383
ISBN 0-398-03734-5

to Nancy and Kathryn, our wives; Kenda, Kris, and Yvonne, our children; and to the many colleagues, friends, and students who have shared so much of themselves in making this contribution possible.

FOREWORD

To offer the potential reader a balanced overview of Nexus Psychotherapy, we have asked that both a humanist and a behaviorist respond to what we have done. Thus, the first part of the Foreword was written by Dr. Howard Rosenblatt, and the second part of the Foreword was written by Dr. Harold Dawley.

Dr. Rosenblatt, who is the author of many existential works including two recent publications, *Some Philosophical Aspects of the Peak Experience* and *The Humanness of Two Abrahams,* had this to say about the book:

ALTHOUGH WHAT I SAY can generally be addressed to both authors, I must say that, when Ken Gutsch asked Harold Dawley and me (two of his former students) to write the foreword for *Nexus Psychotherapy,* I thought, "This is so typical of Ken to share his creativity and joy with his students." Harold and I, because of our different professional orientations, view his book from different perspectives; however, the marvelous thing is that Harold, who is oriented toward the behavioristic point of view, and I, oriented in existential-humanistic attitudes, can, as a result of reading this book, learn more about our respective professional areas. In addition, and even more important, we come to understand each other much better than before. Isn't this what nexus psychotherapy is all about. . .people finding a link between their own world and that of others?

Those interested in the humanistic aspects of *Nexus Psychotherapy* will find the dialogue exciting. At times, the therapist appears to be confused (human?) and attempts to achieve cognitive clarity for both the patient and therapist. The attitude of "What I'm hearing is thus and so, but you also seem to be saying something else. I'm confused. Can you explain this difference?" creates a state of dissonance (and also the opportunity for creative thinking and feeling). The patient may move toward seeking closure through risk or attempt to play it safe by the avoidance

vii

of risk. Shakespeare's "to be or not to be" is the question clearly at stake here. The therapist presses (risks?) and observes the other's idiosyncratic movements. There is a process going on within and between two people with each moving toward closure and greater identity. Each finds more identity (essence?) as a result of such risking. The reciprocity in the relationship at times involves fusion (closure) of a very special nature, based not in technique but purely in an I-Thou attitude. Many other stimulating humanistic considerations are found in the book. Of equal fascination is the attempt to use behavioristic concepts to clarify the dynamics in the process of dialogue. The scientific emphasis given to understanding such dynamics, *e.g.* through the use of computer-type flow charts, seems to relate to the fondest hopes as expressed by the late Abraham Maslow.

Nexus Psychotherapy must, therefore, be a very special book, one which excites a so-called humanistic psychologist like me to find fascination in behavioristic considerations. I suspect that Dr. Dawley finds the humanistic aspects in the book to be very thought-provoking, too.

Leave it to Ken Gutsch to link the two of us together, a "behaviorist" and a "humanist," giving *him* a sense of closure and great satisfaction!

HOWARD S. ROSENBLATT

Dr. Dawley, the author of many works on behavior including two recent publications, *Self-Directed Systematic Desensitization* and the *Patient's Manual for Systematic Desensitization,* commented as follows:

Nexus Psychotherapy is a creative endeavor which evolved from humanistic, phenomenological, and behavorial approaches to psychotherapy. It reflects a rich background of therapeutic understanding as well as an interesting approach to theory. Approaching psychotherapy from a reconstructive point of view, the authors have introduced a process-oriented approach to psychotherapy which seeks to remediate faulty or unadaptive perceptions, beliefs, and/or attitudes while, at the same time, modifying unadaptive behavior. In approaching psychotherapy this way, the authors bring to this book a unique view of the psychotherapeutic process and present the reader with a provocative and stimulating model. In view of the large number of different conceptualizations of psychotherapy, I found the research in the last chapter of the book consistent with the growing emphasis on validating techniques and procedures labeled *psychotherapy*.

Students, therapists, clients, and others reading this book will find it an enriching experience. Nexus psychotherapy is a new addition to the psychotherapeutic vocabulary and, in my opinion, will be around for some time.

HAROLD H. DAWLEY, JR.

PREFACE

NEXUS PSYCHOTHERAPY is an approach involving an extensive network of therapeutically significant interconnections or links not only between humanism and behaviorism but between what a person perceives and the reality of what exists. While both of these areas of synthesis are significant in their own right, it is our conviction that nexus psychotherapy's most important contribution may well be attributed to two basic philosophical and theoretical foundations. The first is a working rapprochement of humanism and behaviorism. This pragmatic "common-law marriage" of widely divergent yet expediently compatible partners has long been hoped for by psychotherapists.

Second, nexus psychotherapy provides a comprehensive orientation to professional relating that takes into account the whole person. We believe that man is more than a living machine, *i.e.* a system of receptors (sense organs) attached to levers (bones) and fueling and controlling organs such as the stomach and glands (Bigge, 1964).

It is also our contention that man is more than a passive creature in a totally deterministic environment of atomistic s-r bonds. Yet, it seems essential that we recognize these partial qualities as real. As such, they provide us with useful conceptual tools, even though they may not be totally descriptive of man.

Conversely, it is also necessary to recognize the fact that man is more than a collection of introspective human experiences. Obviously, he operates from his own interpretations of reality—a fact which, in and by itself, tells us that he is covertly shaped by subtle contingencies of which he is consciously unaware. The principal point is that man seems to be best defined by a combination of behavioral and mentalistic concepts. That is, man cannot be exclusively delegated to either separate theoretical viewpoint, *i.e.* humanism or behaviorism.

In providing a rational and pragmatic bridge toward combining these schools of thought, nexus psychotherapy attempts to consider and treat the whole man. That is, it deals with both his attitudinal and perceptual frame of reference as well as his coping strategies and those potentially forceful environmental factors which operate in shaping his life-style.

CONTENTS

		Page
Preface	**Nexus Psychotherapy**	xi

Chapter

1	**Introduction**	3
	What is Nexus Psychotherapy?	3
	How does Nexus Psychotherapy Differ from Other Schools of Therapy?	5
	How is Nexus Psychotherapy Implemented?	6

2	**Nexus Psychotherapy: A Link Between Two Worlds of Thought**	10
	The Nature of Man	10
	Psychotherapy Defined	14
	Man: In Search for Identity	15
	Learning and Behavior Change	16
	Nexus Psychotherapy as a Theory	16
	Festinger's Dissonance Theory	36
	The Role of the Therapist	36

3	**Schematic Analysis of Nexus Psychotherapy Through Algorithm**	38
	Algorithmic Schematization	38
	Flowchart Language	39
	Learning in Nexus Theory	42
	Nexus Therapy for Type I Problems	47
	Nexus Therapy for Type II Problems	56

4	**Nexus Psychotherapy as an Art of Relating**	64
	The Case of Mat	65
	Risk: The Key to Change	75
	Metalanguage: A Key to Understanding	81

Chapter   *Page*

  5 **Nexus Psychotherapy as a Science of Understanding** 84
     Depression as a Coping Strategy 84
     The Press Technique 85
     Implementing Behavior Change 87
     The Therapist's Role 89
     The Nexus Therapist in Action 98
     The Application of Treatment Techniques 100
     Transcript Segments 101
     Schematic Interpretation 108
     Pattern Formation 108

  6 **Nexus Psychotherapy: Other Movements and Coping**
     Strategies 112
     The Case of Denny 112
     Moving Toward People 129
     The Case of Paul 129
     Research 135

  7 **Exploring the Effectiveness of Nexus Psychotherapy**
     Through Research 137
     Some Speculations About Relating and Research 138
     Testing New Ideas Through Research 141
     The ESC: Interrater Reliability and Intrarater Stability .. 143
     Emotional Stress Characteristics: Training for Recognition 146
     Instructions for Using the ESC 148
     ESC Movement and Q-Sort Results 151
     Plotting Self-Actualizing Tendencies 151
     Results of the Study 157
     Control Group Analysis 158
     Conclusions 165
     Discussion 167

     Bibliography 172
     Index 177

NEXUS PSYCHOTHERAPY

CHAPTER 1

INTRODUCTION

NEXUS PSYCHOTHERAPY is a reconstructive psychotherapy based on the idea that people are constantly searching for greater self-direction. The process by which they search becomes the construct by which they live. When the construct leads to difficulty, it is because the process by which it was formed has been contaminated. Ultimately, the challenge to such contamination is the extent to which the process can be reconstructed to close the gap between what one anticipates and the reality of what truly exists.

To provide the reader with an introductory overview of how nexus psychotherapy might compare with other approaches to psychotherapy, the authors have posed three questions:

1. What is nexus psychotherapy?
2. How does it differ from other schools of psychotherapy?
3. How is it implemented?

The answers to these questions should give the reader a basic understanding of the approach taken by the authors and the theoretical premise upon which the book is based.

WHAT IS NEXUS PSYCHOTHERAPY?

Nexus psychotherapy is a process-oriented approach to understanding human relations. By definition, nexus means *link*. Perhaps one of the best illustations of how such a link can be defined is given by Milhollan and Forisha in their book, *From Skinner to Rogers* (1972). In talking about psychotherapy, they say that analysis begins with the situation or experience as it is given. Accordingly, therefore, the word *phenomena* is defined as that which is perceived. Ultimately, what is perceived is contrasted with that which is real. This is not to imply that what you perceive is not real, but only that there can be a difference between what you perceive and the reality of what exists. Carl Rogers (1961) referred to man's ability to link an experience with an awareness of that experience as congruence. What this means in theory is that, if there is a split between what one perceives and the reality of what truly exists, such a situation can be defined as potentially stressful.

Actually, it now appears that there are a number of conditions which lead to such a split. One such condition is the conflict between where a person wants to go and the method he uses to get there, *i.e.* between his objectives in life and his life process. Some people seem to have difficulty understanding that the methods they are using to reach their objectives are in conflict with the objectives they seek. One illustration of this might be the young man who wants to date but avoids contact with women. Another illustration might be the student who wants to become a medical doctor but refuses to take science courses.

A second incongruency which seems rather prominent among individuals who experience stress is the split between what a person experiences and how he responds to that experience. That is, the employee who wants to tell his boss to go to hell but instead compliments everything his boss does. These splits between what a person says and what he thinks or between his objectives and the method he uses to reach them are self-defeating for they destroy the person's potential for personal identity. Because the basis from which he works is not entirely real, he becomes uncertain about his self-direction. This uncertainty, in turn, becomes the basis for stress. His search, therefore, concerns itself with how to deal with stress more effectively. The methods by which he does this are recognized as coping strategies. Coping strategies are neither "good" nor "bad," they are simply components of a systematic pattern a person follows when attempting to reach an objective. If they work, they are usually strengthened and repeated. If they do not work, the person who is trying them usually experiences pressure, frustration, and conflict.

In both of these examples, there is a serious split between the person's perception of the experience and the reality of how the experience is treated in terms of objectives and procedures. All such splits, it seems, illustrate a lack of closure (Allport, 1937), which is the ability on the part of the perceiver to understand how his experiences can become integrated into his total life-style—how his experiences can become a comfortable and meaningful part of his life.

Each time a person fails to reach those objectives he has set for himself, he loses that personal identity which tells him that he understands how to deal effectively with his life. His search, therefore, is to find out how he relates to the world around him. Within this world, nexus psychotherapy is simply an approach to relating which helps a client find identity and improve the way he organizes his life. The method by which this is accomplished involves linking what the person perceives with the reality of what truly exists. It is a means by which the person learns to deal with the reality of the situation in which he finds himself, and it is the vehicle by which he learns to understand experiences and how to make the most of those experiences, regardless of the consequences.

HOW DOES NEXUS PSYCHOTHERAPY DIFFER FROM OTHER SCHOOLS OF THERAPY?

Nexus psychotherapy is a process-oriented therapy. What this means is that, in nexus psychotherapy, man is viewed neither as a totally dependent nor a totally independent variable. That is, he is seen as neither totally molded by his environment and shaped by his experiences nor totally independent of such forces. In practice, it seems that man is actually as Maine de Brian saw him, *i.e.* a person who not only has an impact on his environment but is also impacted by his environment.

Although the arguments posed by Skinner (1965), Eysenck (1959), Wolpe (1958), May (1960), Buytendijk (1950), and Rogers (1959) are all quite impressive, it is our opinion that behavior can be changed by outside forces such as shaping *and* by inner forces such as synergism (Goble, 1971).

Obviously, these forces are part of man's struggle with autonomy. They reflect both his desire to be free to make decisions and his desire to follow an available model. Both determine, to some degree, the type of personal identity with which he must live. Whether or not the decisions he makes have been shaped by his previous experiences or synergized by a process of ingestion is perhaps of less importance than the fact that the outcome of this blending of internal and external forces becomes the basis for the process by which man lives. Ultimately, it is man's process which becomes the dependent variable, for it is his process which is formed and shaped by the interaction of these forces, and it is his process by which he moves through life. Thus, nexus psychotherapy differs from other schools of thought in that it accepts man as both an independent and a dependent variable; it sees him as dependent when he is being shaped or molded by other forces, yet recognizes that he can synergize what he has learned and reach beyond his present moment of existence into a completely different world. We also recognize that his ability to synergize is not always active, just as an athlete may not always perform at his peak level. Yet, the potential for such action is there.

The significance of using process orientation as a constant suffers at least one major criticism. Since man has the potential to change at any time, what assurance do we have that his process is not constantly changing? Our response to this question is simply this: By understanding the process by which man makes changes, we already understand his variability for change. Perhaps a more descriptive way of phrasing this would be to say that, if you want to know where a person is going, simply look at where he has been (Super, 1954), or if you want to understand man, simply analyze his process of behavior and those intentions which define it (Sartre, 1953).

HOW IS NEXUS PSYCHOTHERAPY IMPLEMENTED?

The key to implementing nexus psychotherapy rests with the therapist's ability to challenge his client's present interpretation of an experience in terms of the reality of the situation which exists. It is the contention of the authors that successful therapy is possible only when the person understands the structure of his existence and is challenged to find his way back to reality by searching for truth, participating in it as he finds it and relating to it as he experiences it. To accomplish this end, the nexus psychotherapist works with what is behaviorally real to his client as well as what is physically observable to the therapist.

Nexus psychotherapy, therefore, differs from other schools of thought in that it is a two-step approach to therapy. First, it recognizes that values, interests, and anticipations are attitudinal. It accepts as a basic premise the idea that whatever changes are to be made through psychotherapy will probably first be made on an attitudinal level and then reality tested.

Second, it subscribes to the idea that, after man formulates interpretations of his experiences, he then responds in terms of what he feels will be in his best interests. Thus, what he does in practice is to interpret an experience and then work out a method of operation which is related to getting for him whatever it is he wants. This method is composed of coping strategies or moves he makes to accomplish his objectives. As an example, he may laugh when someone is aggressive in order to deal with aggression. Although he feels no humor, he has learned that laughing sometimes neutralizes aggressiveness. When the method takes him some place other than where he wants to go and he cannot see any alternatives which are less threatening or more meaningful than what he is already doing, then he may feel pressure, experience frustration, or anticipate conflict.

In nexus psychotherapy, then, there are two types of problems: a Type I problem, which deals with how a person perceives or interprets an experience and a Type II problem, which deals with how a person responds to an experience. Thus, if a person's interpretation of an experience is faulty, his method of responding will also be faulty. By "faulty," we mean that, since he does not have all the facts, he cannot utilize his coping strategies as well as he wants to and, as a result, experiences a lack of congruency between where he is going and how he intends to get there or between what he says and what he feels.

Over a period of years, these strategies become habituated and can very easily be identified as patterns which define the person's life-style. To determine such patterns, and carry out therapy, certain steps seem essential:

a. First, the therapist must listen to the client and determine what his patterns of relating are like, *i.e.* how well his coping strategies work, how he makes decisions, how he responds to failure, how well his process for reaching his objective works, how receptive he seems to change, and how willing he seems to risk himself in an effort to bring about change.

b. Second, the therapist must determine which of these patterns leads to the frustration, conflict, or pressure his client is experiencing. Once the therapist understands these patterns, part of his therapeutic responsibility will be to challenge the client each time he approaches the set patterns which carry him to the outcomes he does not want.

c. Third, in order to break up these patterns, the nexus therapist uses a method called a press technique. One method of pressing is referred to as "perceptual chipping." To perceptually chip is to challenge a client's present interpretation of an experience by encouraging him to look at what he is doing in terms of the reality of the consequences which might result.

d. Fourth, the therapist frequently goes beyond perceptual chipping and uses a more sophisticated press technique referred to as "juxtapositioning," *i.e.* comparing the reality of contrasting thoughts by bringing such thoughts together so that the person can reflect on what those contrasts mean. One way of doing this is to contrast the methods used by the client with the reality of the consequences they bring.

e. Fifth, as a result of such therapeutic intervention, the client reaches a point where he realizes that, to move ahead in life, he must risk what he has against alternatives he felt were impossible before therapy was implemented.

f. Sixth, as a condition to risking, the client must understand the consequences of what he is about to do; he must deal with the reality of failure and how it can be converted into success.

Caught between his intentions to reach certain objectives and the demands of societal forces which govern his progress, each person must decide how he can best survive. Obviously, he seeks both to appease himself and his society, but unfortunately, this is not always possible. When he cannot appease both, he rationalizes his position by entering a twilight zone where incongruency becomes primary, and harmony, secondary. The method by which he moves is a pattern. It is nurtured by time and subscribes to the values, interests, and anticipations which govern his life-style. Ultimately, these patterns tell us not only where he was but where he will probably go. If his perception is faulty, if it consists of faulty interpretations, misunderstandings, inaccuracies, or anticipations, then his patterns of responding will also be faulty, and as a result, he will experience stress.

One of the most intriguing factors to which the nexus psychotherapist addresses himself is his client's uniqueness. In nexus psychotherapy, each person is recognized as both consistently unique (Mischel, 1977) and uniquely consistent (Sartre, 1953). What this means in practice is that each person is different from all other people in some ways, yet repeats himself with such consistency that he becomes highly predictable in other ways. Ultimately, it is the consistency with which he repeats himself that establishes the basis by which he is understood. In this sense, his patterning actually becomes a delicate blending of cognitive styling (Grebstein, 1969) and operant level functioning (Skinner, 1975). That is to say that what is learned is not only a set of responses but an internal strategy by which the responses are put into action, *i.e.* coping strategies (Chomsky, 1959; Beach, Hebb, Morgan, and Nissen, 1960; Ritchie, Aeschliman, and Pierce, 1950; Kretchevsky, 1932).

CHAPTER 2

NEXUS PSYCHOTHERAPY: A Link
Between Two Worlds of Thought

Intro-

FOR YEARS, THEORISTS have viewed humanism and behaviorism as two approaches to psychotherapy which are diametrically opposed (Osipow, 1970; Eysenck, 1966). Many of the discussions generated by these two schools of thought have dealt with the feasibility of researching the effectiveness of psychotherapy. While the former school of thought subscribes to the ideal that the constructive forces which alter perception reside primarily within the individual (Rogers, 1951), the latter school advocates the idea that, to change a person's behavior, you must first change his environment (Milhollan and Forisha, 1972). What this means in practice is that, while the humanist concerns himself with a person's attitudes, the behaviorist concerns himself with the conduct which results when a person converts these attitudes into actions. Since both concepts are inseparable parts of a person's total existence, it seems that the foundation from which differences emerge is really more philosophical than scientific. Assuming that this is true, it seems that whatever precedes therapeutic theory must first find its rationale in a more highly definitive philosophy dealing primarily with what man is, *i.e.* the nature of man and how he learns.

THE NATURE OF MAN

Philosophically speaking, man seems to be the product of two ill-defined worlds: his own perceptual internal world and its external environmental counterpart (Goble, 1970). The extent to which these two forces are brought into harmony will, to some degree, determine how well a person functions emotionally. For

10

the most part, what this means is that man is a composite of experiences—not necessarily a collection of static substances (May, 1967) but, rather, a sequence of adventures promoted by a desire to go beyond wherever it is he finds himself. To this end, man is in the process of becoming. Essentially, he is a growing, changing entity. But his growth is not without restriction and structure. His own anticipation of what is yet to come sometimes distorts his reality of what truly exists. Therefore, what exists for him may not be a reality but a distortion based on his anticipations, expectations, or fantasies.

Although what actually goes on in a person's mind is not easily discernible, humanists have long perceived the essence of understanding as attitudinal. To them, experiences which become manifest through response patterns have meant little. It has been their contention that an experience which is not in process is inhibited or repressed. This means that the responsibility of the therapist is to assist his client in dealing with experiences by making these experiences a meaningful part of his total process of functioning. To do this, the therapist and the client search together for causes underlying stress, frustration, conflict, and pressure.

Behaviorists, on the other hand, do not concern themselves with what may or may not be inhibited but deal only with that which is released. It is hypothesized that, by dealing with responses in this way, they help the client to bring his frustration under control by extinguishing or displacing anxiety-inducing stimuli.

Granted that both of these propositions differ theoretically, it still appears that what man experiences and how he responds may have some common ground not yet sufficiently explored. It seems that Don Super touched upon at least one of these commonalities in 1954 when he explained his developmental approach to vocational counseling by defining the thematic extrapolative method by which his procedure was implemented (Super, 1954). He went on to explain that, by observing themes of the past, it was possible to get a fairly accurate impression of what the future would be like. One can hardly imagine Ellis's Rational-Emotive Therapy without some idea of what rational means or Wolpe's Reciprocal Inhibition Psychotherapy without some idea of how hierarchies of fear are defined. In short, all of these therapies use themes to determine where man has been, where he is, or where he is attempting to go.

To understand this commonality, one must also understand the metalanguage by which humanistic therapists can become more pragmatic as they work with people. One example of how metalanguage is communicated in psychotherapy is to listen to the failing student who insists that he "couldn't study for the test because friends insisted that it was better to relax before a test by going to a ball game" or to hear the married woman who insists that her husband is the most wonderful person in the world "... if only he could develop better social manners." Metalanguage is the means by which people confuse the reality of their experiences with the fantasy of their desires. It is an ongoing process by which people temper the reality of "what is" with the anticipation of "what could be." At times, it seems like an excellent way of saying two things at the same time (May, 1960). This conflicting approach to reasoning leads to incongruencies which result in frustration, confusion, and pressure.

The reality of how metalanguage works can be illustrated by a client who complained of a poor memory. After seeing him for a number of weeks, it became obvious to the therapist that his statements were in conflict with his performance. That is, in some areas, his memory seemed rather questionable; in others, it seemed truly good. When, during therapy, the therapist explored with him what purpose a bad memory served, the client suddenly reached a point where he blurted out, "Only fools are always right." To which the therapist responded by saying, "And what, exactly, does that mean?" In exploring his feelings, the client recognized it as a response his mother frequently gave when, as a child, he asked out of curiosity about her nightly visitors. Apparently, his mother denied that she had visitors and, when an argument ensued, would ultimately end up saying, "Only fools are always right." Her purpose was to create some doubt in the mind of the client about his memory. Obviously, her efforts were successful. Her metalanguage was the means by which he brought the lack of closure with his mother into the presence of his therapy.

What this may indicate is that there is no such thing as an experience which is not in process. Nothing is really unconscious, repressed, inhibited, covert, or denied. It is simply a matter of understanding each person well enough to know how he handles his experiences and how he communicates what he understands or how he links his inner frame of reference with his behavioral responses.

One thing which seems apparent is that a person's ability to handle an experience has much to do with his flexibility, *i.e.* his ability to remain psychologically open enough so that his full potential for developing new alternative choices is available to him. Obviously, man is restricted by tunnel vision. If he is not aware of his potential, then he is restricted by his inability to understand what alternatives are available. Some theorists might argue that this is a fatalistic way of looking at life. It would seem, however, that to acknowledge the fact that such restrictive areas of thinking exist is really to acknowledge the purpose behind psychotherapy. If a therapist is actually an agent of change, then it appears that such change might best be implemented when a client is capable of recognizing his potential for change. For most people, it seems that change will come when they are willing to risk themselves; when they are willing to enter into life as equally responsible participants. For many of these people, stress will grow out of feelings which lack reality. Therapy is the means by which such confused people can once again gain that reality.

There is a kind of statistical determination about therapy which dictates that, if a person does a certain thing in a certain way, the probability of getting a specific result will be rather high. Such a concept emerges from the belief that each person acts in a manner which is his by choice, and that, at any given moment, he can make a decision which, in essence, has been selected from among those alternatives he understands as his. To this end, he is an agent of free choice. But, to the extent that his past experiences and his present anticipations play a significant role in this choice, he is somewhat limited. Nevertheless, the responsibility for a choice remains his, as does the method by which he seeks results relative to that choice. Although he may not be capable of seeing all his alternatives, he is obligated by his commitment to himself and his society to seek help in understanding his potential. Naturally, a person is never obligated to do what he does not want to do; it is simply a question of what penalty he is willing to pay as a consequence of remaining the way he is (Arbuckle, 1970). Buford Stefflre once said, "I was never certain about where I wanted to go, but I was always pretty certain about where I did not want to remain" (Stefflre, 1970). It seems that this force within man to move away from what he does not want, plus his desire to move toward those things he does want, serves as the basis for the direction he takes in life. His experiences and anticipations serve as the reservoir from which he draws his direction in life. Each path he takes to reach an objective is probably relegated to meet with as little resistance as possible (Sullivan, 1947). When he cannot reach his objectives or find alternatives, he becomes frustrated.

Rhetorically speaking, one might say that, although man can choose his course in life, he frequently finds himself without the essential equipment to make the trip. What this means is that, even though he may be the captain of his fate, he is certainly not the master of his destiny. His right to choose does not mean that he will have the wisdom necessary to make wise choices or the experience necessary to recognize his full potential.

It is not so much a question of how good a person is, but more a question of what his intentions are and how these intentions are affecting his life. Through nexus therapy, the person will explore this intent and how it relates or is linked to his total life process.

PSYCHOTHERAPY DEFINED

In practice then, psychotherapy serves as a catalyst by which the process of decision making is examined. This delicate method of blending the intrinsic thoughts of man with his feelings about the world in which he lives makes therapy both an art and a science. Seemingly, it emerges from a philosophy of life based on the idea that learning to relate serves as an antecedent to the development of a process of successful living. As an art, it begins with the unique method by which the relationship is formed; as a science, it graduates to an objective and scientific understanding of man gleaned through testing and trained observation. In theory, it recognizes the idea that, whatever man is, he has become and that the process of becoming is an ongoingness which makes man something other than what he was. In practice, it suggests that a special type of helping relationship can serve as the catalyst by which man moves from where he is to where he wants to go.

Pragmatically speaking then, therapy is a point of view which emphasizes professional assistance in meeting the various emotional needs created when people are thrown into, have grown into, or are born into critical situations which pose decision-making and responsibility-taking challenges. It is an experiential process that takes place as individuals are aided in making decisions, interpretations, and adjustments. And it is a concept of relating which becomes manifest through the application of such basic processes as testing, measuring, motivating, analyzing, diagnosing, prognosing, and researching. As a functional approach to understanding through relating, it recognizes man as both a scientific and philosophical entity.

MAN: IN SEARCH FOR IDENTITY

Basically, the person who accepts new experiences and challenges is seen as one who is going out from himself in an effort to grow. His desire to integrate his experiences and make them a meaningful part of his life serves as the stimulus which causes him to explore new ideas. It is this curiosity about life and how it relates to his total ability to function that continues to inspire him to work toward closure. Closure is the resolution of an experience; it is man's ability to bring an experience into his total system of functioning and understand the role it plays in that system. Personality is the unique pattern of behavior he acquires as he struggles with those elements which resist closure; behavior change is the process by which his patterns of responding are altered, and learning is the process by which his thinking about alternatives is enhanced.

Ultimately, closure serves as a means to identity. It helps the person understand how he fits into the world around him. It helps him to understand how each step he takes in life will, for an eternity that is yet to come, let others know that he was here, *i.e.* it provides a delicate linking of his response repertoire with the unique meaning it holds for him. It also helps him to understand that his life is simply an intrusion into a world which is virtually insensitive to his presence, not necessarily because he is not important but, rather, because each person experiences the impact of his own search and, therefore, does not, or perhaps cannot, concern himself primarily with the struggles of others.

LEARNING AND BEHAVIOR CHANGE

It is as man searches for this identity that he must make some decisions about where he is going and how he can get there. Because of his past experiences and his present anticipations, he frequently selects those avenues of life which seem to provide the greatest promise. When his decisions are poor, he attempts to change the consequences; when they are good, he attempts to sustain the method by which he was successful. As he exhausts his alternatives, he becomes a person in trouble. It is as he experiences such trouble or becomes confused concerning the variety of decisions he has to make that he sometimes seeks help. The person to whom he goes, at least in some instances, will be a psychotherapist. If, as a result of therapy his behavior changes, then therapy has served as a learning process (Mowrer, 1948; Ullman, 1945). What he learns will be reinforced positively by the extent to which he can reality test such changes with satisfaction to himself and benefit to society. Thus, therapy becomes the *sine qua non* by which man realizes his potential as a totally functioning person and his deficiencies as a partially functioning person.

NEXUS PSYCHOTHERAPY AS A THEORY

To develop a theoretical basis by which therapy can be understood and taught, it is essential to understand that a theory, if it is to be inclusive, must deal with man both as an actor within his environment and a reactor to his environment. That is, it must deal with those patterns by which man's uniqueness is characterized as well as those coping strategies by which he moves toward, away from, or against potential life experiences.

Theory, if it is to be communicated in a meaningful way, must also deal with the concept of multiple determination, the idea that events do not result from random and isolated causes but emerge out of an orderly and logical sequence of complex influences. To do this, theorists must consider both the experimental approach, which attempts to establish a cause-effect relationship through the manipulation and control of variables, and the naturalistic approach, which observes variables in their natural settings and then correlates or links these variables together in accord with their pattern of interaction.

The major problem with experimental control settings is that they are often artificial and produce designs in which the number and nature of variables available for study are limited. Naturalistic approaches, on the other hand, permit the researcher to analyze a complex of naturally interacting variables without intervening controls or manipulations. These are approaches based on the belief that one can hope to find a law by including the total organism in observations and experiences. (Millon, 1967)

Essentially, there are two naturalistic approaches, one is intuitive and qualitative; the other is objective and quantitative The first uses case histories, clinical observation, and interviews; the second uses multivariate methods in which all variables are measured rather than observed. In the latter case, computers are used to abstract those regularities which exist.

One of the advantages to nexus psychotherapy is that it uses a thematic extrapolative approach (Super, 1964) which links the patterns of where a person has been with the reality of where he is attempting to go, *i.e.* it recognizes that one way of determining what a person will do in the future is to understand what he did in the past. In other words, it links an individual's thematic past to his present, always keeping a vigilant watch on how that theme must be modified if behavior is to change for the better. To this extent, it is naturalistic, intuitive, and qualitative, for it recognizes that what one did in the past can be postulated (hypothesized) by analyzing the sequence of events which precede any recurrent themes. The consistency with which such themes or patterns occur defines a person's predisposition toward specific values, attitudes, interests, or desires (Super, 1954, Gutsch and Peters, 1973).

Nexus psychotherapy especially recognizes two human aspects:

> (1) behavior as an organized pattern of responding to experiences and
> (2) learning as the process of utilizing experiences in ways which provide alternatives not possible before the experiences occurred.

Further, it recognizes emotional stress as an inability on the part of a person to adjust to the condition he experiences; it creates within him a lack of understanding about who he is, what he wants to do, or where he wants to go. Thus, stress becomes an inefficient way of thinking and reasoning sometimes caused by confusion, conflict, frustration, or pressure. Such conditions inhibit the effectiveness of the person and cause some concern about how he relates to society. Thus, according to nexus psychotherapy, the way learning takes place is this:

> (1) A person interacts with his environment. As he does so, he is both affected by and affects the environment of which he is a part.
> (2) The person integrates into his system those experiences which are compatible with the system and displaces those which are incompatible.
> (3) Experiences, both compatible and incompatible, influence the person and cause him to respond in specific ways.
> (4) The unique patterns of reaction developed by the person under these conditions are responses of convenience and may or may not serve in the best interests of the self-sought objectives of the person.
> (5) Patterns can be altered by the person through changed attitude and/or changed environment.

(6) Changes by the person, at best, serve him tentatively for they emerge from a life cycle which demands adaptation to new and varied experiences.

This means that man is neither a totally dependent variable nor a totally independent variable. That is, it appears that his behavior is neither totally dependent on his environment nor totally independent of his environment. Actually, he not only has an impact on his environment but is impacted by his environment.

David Ausubel (1957) has theorized that one cannot rationalize that, just because a person's behavior changes every time the situational context is altered, his change is determined by the latter variable alone. In fact, by stabilizing the situational context and varying the people exposed to it, one could emerge with the equally faulty conclusion that only personality factors determine behavioral change.

Obviously, behavior is a difficult subject to explore, not only because it is highly complex, but because it is a process. It is evanescent, changing, and elusive. Yet, when it represents itself habitually, it can also be treated as a constant. Knowing what a person has done in the past offers a high probability of predicting what he might do in the future (Kluckhohn and Murray, 1948).

In essence then, nexus psychotherapy represents an empirical and theoretical rapprochement of humanistic and behavioristic concepts and becomes a means by which these two major schools of thought can be linked together to become the pragmatic basis for a much-needed change in psychotherapy. It is an approach which is geared to help a person understand how each experience can best serve his adaptation cycle; in other words, how a person can benefit from each experience regardless of whether, at first appearance, it seems to be "good" or "bad." It is a concept which deals with the way a person relates both to himself and to the world around him. Most important, however, is the idea that it pragmatically incorporates the twilight zone between humanism and behaviorism and makes it possible for the therapist to deal with the process by which a person and his experiential feelings are blended into self-internalized ideas about living, *i.e.* making decisions, holding values, and forming attitudes.

As a process-oriented approach to therapy, nexus psychotherapy concerns itself with two problems: a Type I and a Type II. Definitively speaking, a Type I problem is based on attitudes observable through topical patterns reflected by a person as he interrelates with his therapist. It serves as the basis from which the person makes decisions, forms values, expresses attitudes, and explores interests. A Type II problem deals with the method of operation or process followed by the person as he responds to experiences based on these values, interests, and attitudes. Naturally, how a person interprets an experience, how he tests it against reality, and how much, if any, concern he has for the safety of his personal identity while reality testing is going on, makes a difference that for each individual is unique.

Obviously, a person who becomes overly concerned about losing his identity will hesitate to trust himself as a decision maker. It is as a person becomes true to himself and responds to an experience honestly rather than out of fantasy or fear that he begins to see himself as having personal identity. The process by which he makes such decisions and follows through to reach self-sought objectives is known as risking. His ability to risk will, it seems (Gutsch and Mueller, 1975), determine how other decisions are made and how he will view himself as a decision maker. Ultimately, it is this attitude toward himself and how well he functions which serves the person as the basis for his behavior.

The two basic problems with which therapy must concern itself are (a) understanding what a person is experiencing and (b) understanding his intentions in responding. Both are process oriented. The first involves a process of dealing with an experience attitudinally; the second, a process of responding to that experience functionally. Theoretically, the idea is that, if the process of arriving at an attitude is faulty, then the method of responding to the attitude will also be faulty.

Ultimately, one purpose of any therapy is to get a person to understand where he is and how he got there. For the behaviorist, such an understanding may come from building hierarchies and helping a person to understand that whatever he does is simply a reflection of what he has learned. For the humanist, it serves as the basis for attitudinal change through insight. Within the realm of nexus therapy, such understandings are designed to bring about change by helping the person to examine the incongruencies between such things as (a) his objectives and the process by which he is attempting to reach those objectives, and/or (b) his perception of an experience and the reality of the experience.

Much of the change, if any, which is brought about through therapy will be the result of successful reality testing on the part of the person. His attitude will change when he finds that he can accomplish previously established objectives through new understandings and/or different approaches. Conversely, when it is difficult for a person to base his decisons on reality, he will frequently resort to fantasy. As a result, his fantasy-based direction (his method of operation) will be faulty; the basis from which he works will lead him into greater difficulty than he already experiences. At moments like this, his failure is more closely related to his faulty anticipation of an experience than to the reality of that experience. Ultimately, he responds through a faulty method of operation simply because he perceives in a faulty manner. Over a period of time, this habituated method—in this case, a negative reciprocal chain reaction—becomes difficult to overcome without therapy, and as a result, the person's faulty process of decision making compounds the difficulties, pressures, frustrations, and confusions he experiences. Perhaps one of the best ways of thinking about a therapy which draws from both the areas of humanism and behaviorism is to think about it as an approach which not only concerns itself with etiologies and symptoms, but also with processes by which such etiologies are nurtured and through which such symptoms become manifest.

When working with clients, this operational procedure for drawing from both areas of humanism and behaviorism involves the following:

(1) Attitudinally exploring with the client the nature of the interactions between himself and his environment.
(2) Utilizing this exploration to determine what, if any, incongruencies exist between what the client feels about his experiences and the way he responds to them.

(3) Working with the client to discover those features of his attitude and his environment which sustain the reinforcement patterns which cause him concern.

(4) Exploring with the client those areas of his attitude which seem most receptive to change and the formation of new alternatives.

(5) Reality testing the feasibility of pursuing new alternatives.

(6) Exploring the possibilities of converting attitudinal changes into reality through a process which brings satisfaction to one's self and benefit to society.

In assisting a person to reach a level where he can risk, *i.e.* assert himself, nexus psychotherapy draws from both the areas of behaviorism and humanism through the utilization of these six basic steps:

(1) Modeling relaxation.

(2) Examining patterns of reaction (themes).

(3) Examining coping strategies and the metalanguage by which they are communicated.

(4) Computing units of emotional stress.

(5) Implementing a press technique through the use of "perceptual chipping," juxtaposition, and recapitulation.

(6) Reality-testing changing attitudes.

Identification is the process by which a person takes over the features of another person and incorporates them into his own personality. The person whom he emulates is the model. The method by which he is understood is definitive, and the process by which life patterns become manifest is thematic extrapolative.

Modeling Relaxation

Modeling Relaxation involves five basic steps:

(1) *Listening.* Listening is an indication of the therapist's commitment to his client. By listening very carefully, the nexus therapist models respect and sensitivity. Listening is also the means by which the nexus therapist develops an awareness of what the client is saying in terms of the reality of what he is doing. In this sense, it serves to define the

reference axis from which the client's cognitive style emerges. Such an understanding helps to establish a basis by which the therapist can juxtapose what the client perceives against the reality of what exists.

(2) *Learned Controls.* Among the greatest instruments the therapist has are his voice and his composure. Through appropriate utilization of these instruments, it is possible for him to model responsibility and maturity. By so doing, he not only creates a climate in which the client feels safe, but one in which the client begins to understand how to provide the conditions of a "better" relationship outside of therapy, *i.e.* how he can generalize what he has learned to other relationships.

(3) *Viewing Incongruencies Tactfully.* Part of modeling relaxation requires that the client explore his phenomenal realities, his perceptual experiences and bring them into harmony with reality. This is an exercise in juxtaposition which helps the client to explore the incongruencies between what he perceives and what actually exists. Modeling takes place as the sharp contrast between methods and goals is explored and the client begins to test the change against reality. At this point, he frequently uses the therapist as a model because he has no other frame of reference from which to draw.

(4) *Risking.* Ultimately, the client reaches a point where he has to risk in order to grow. To do this, he tests what he has learned in his relationship with his therapist against the reality of his encounter with the world around him. Although he at first may lean toward the therapist's world, his apprehension about his own personal identity creates a desire to achieve some assertiveness, thus causing him to risk finding out who he really is. Each time this happens, the impact of modeling becomes the residue of reality testing, for it is displaced by the client's desire to become his own person.

(5) Finally, the ability of the client to become his own person depends on the therapist's attitude toward the relationship.

When the therapist is completely himself in the relationship, the client recognizes that he can become completely
himself. To this extent, modeling is not something the
therapist does, it is something he is—not because he chose
to be a model, but because someone chose him as a model.

The idea of the therapist as a model becomes significant only
as the client draws from him in an effort to find his own identity.
In many ways, it is like the parent who takes his child's hand and
guides him through the formative years of his life. At that
moment, the parent controls the relationship because of the child's
desire for the security of that relationship. As the child grows
older, he eventually reaches a point where he seeks his own
identity, *i.e.* the opportunity to test against reality those things he
has learned from his parents. As he finds success, he innovates to
find his own personal identity. When his attempts to relate fail
and he cannot become autonomous, he is usually in trouble.
Therapy is simply one means by which he deals with such trouble.
Through nexus psychotherapy, he learns how to relate to the
world around him and how to weave his potential for new experiences into a meaningful method of functioning.

To this extent, it might be said that, while the client is using
the psychotherapist as a model, he is actually in the process of
seeking his own personal identity. To find such identity, he incorporates some of what he finds in his therapist into his own
system of functioning. He does this because he has areas of deficiency and does not understand how to respond to such deficiencies. Imitating the therapist until he can discover his own
unique identity seems logical to him because it permits him the
latitude necessary to explore his potential for becoming.

The significance of modeling should probably be viewed not so
much in terms of what the therapist has given the client as it is in
terms of what the client has borrowed from him in an attempt to
find a new and better method of relating outside of therapy.
Then too, it is never so much what belongs to the therapist as it is
what the client can do to transcend this model and become his
own person.

In all of these steps, relaxation is the key to combating anxiety.

Since anxiety and relaxation are antagonistic and, therefore, incompatible, it appears that, if a client is relaxed, he cannot experience anxiety at the same time. The immediate challenge for the therapist is to create a climate in which relaxation is possible and anxiety is remote. To accomplish this end, the therapist must work toward getting his client to relax as he examines the reality of his past experiences. As the client relaxes, the therapist begins a process of perceptual chipping. It is based on the idea that a person sometimes acts in ways which are not readily acceptable simply because his perception of an experience is not accurate. Therapy is the *sine qua non* by which he comes up with new alternative methods of responding.

Studying Patterns of Reaction (Themes)

Most clients will gravitate toward specific topic areas which seem extremely important to them. In most cases, these topic areas form patterns involving relationships and concepts. Many times, such patterns seem to serve as an extension of feelings from the past which were not resolved. This lack of closure created by an inability to resolve such problems causes the client to dwell on them obsessively, hoping always as he does so that he will discover some way to deal with them. That is, he does not understand his problem well enough to control it, nor does he understand it well enough to deal with it. As a result, he becomes frustrated, experiences conflict about what he should do, and feels pressure because of his inability to resolve it.

Examining Coping Strategies

As each theme or pattern is repeated, it reveals to a certain degree how the client is dealing with basic life issues. Each pattern is, therefore, an area within which the client's basic coping strategies are revealed. In his book, *The Divided Self,* Ronald Laing (1969) infers that these strategies are behaviors the patient invents in order to live in an unlivable situation. It can be hypothesized that the client does this either to survive the impact of experiences from which he cannot escape or to avoid experiences with which he cannot deal. In order to cope, each client probably has three basic moves which are possible: moving toward people, moving away from people, or moving against people (Horney, 1942).

Typically, these three moves seem to emerge in the form of three syndromes:

(1) THE DISPIRITED SYNDROME. This is a syndrome character-
    ized by people who are attempting to cope with frustration
    and stress by moving away from others. Typically, they
    have little or no interest in setting goals. They avoid goal
    setting because they want to avoid the failure sometimes in-
    curred when attempting to reach such goals. This is not to
    say that they do not have goals, but only that they do not
    make these goals obvious because they fear failure. To
    avoid the impression of failure, they complain about such
    things as an inability to concentrate. They cushion failure
    by projecting the blame. This is their metalanguage.
    What they want to convey is the idea that they should not
    be held responsible for their work because they just could
    not concentrate, did not have the time, or had too many
    interruptions.

    They seem to dwell on how poorly the past has gone
    and refuse to make decisions because, in the past, decision
    making frequently led to critical evaluation and feelings of
    failure.

    Many of them feel useless. Some feel that death would
    be better. Occasionally, they say things like, "What I'm do-
    ing is of no significance to anyone. I may as well be dead."

    Some react physically and experience a loss of appetite,
    marked nervousness, and excessive fatigue. Others simply
    withdraw and cleverly attempt to get parents, friends, and
    therapists to make decisions for them. If the therapist is
    naive enough to make such decisions, then the therapist
    becomes a "cushion" for failure, and the client can blame
    him for everything.

(2) THE RIGID SYNDROME. This is a syndrome characterized by
    people who are attempting to cope with life by moving
    against others. They are extremely rigid people who

build security walls of meticulousness and perfection in order to avoid making mistakes. They are methodical and exacting in everything they do. The severity of their structuring is, they feel, their method for avoiding failure. Because they feel insecure even within their structure, they frequently project their structure into the world around them. By doing this, they touch other people's lives. Many times, they intrude themselves into the lives of others. This is an attempt to control their environment. What they want is complete control of their lives. One way of getting such control is by building their own world and attempting to control everyone in it.

When a person uses such structuring for himself without intruding himself into the world of others, then he is probably performing at a high level of efficiency. When he intrudes his structuring into the worlds of others, he frequently finds that structuring is not working as he had planned and he begins to feel depressed. Many times when he feels this way, his attempts to control his environment will become more compulsive. If he is unsuccessful (and he usually is), his depression will increase. When he finally reaches a point where he is unable to make a decision about how to move, then he will experience anxiety.

Many times he will worry over trifles; he will become submissive in an effort to gain support for his beliefs and constructs. Other times, he will shift the blame for failure by projecting the blame to someone else. In his work, he is usually critical and frequently becomes the attacker. To attack is to keep his opponents off guard. His rationale seems to be that those who are being attacked cannot attack. It is his way of coping with life and instituting a climate of safety.

His actions in life are really reactions to fear. He sometimes attempts to control the world around him by getting his audience to play the game of life by his rules. Unfortunately, even then his fears seem to continue simply because he does not believe in himself.

(3) THE DRAMATIC SYNDROME. This is a syndrome characterized by people who are attempting to cope with life by moving toward others. Seemingly, they are warm, friendly people who gain the attention of others by moving toward them. Typically, they seek attention, behave seductively, and react dramatically.

Their lives consist of masking, role playing, and imitating. Some of them actually gravitate toward the theater for a livelihood. This is a place where they can take on the identity of the characters they play.

Traditionally, such clients have a flair for drama even when they are not theatrically inclined. Their typical reflections of personal warmth, lightheartedness, and flexibility are lost in any in-depth relationship because there is always a shallowness in the way they relate. Listeners feel that these people are superficial and unable to become an integrated part of the reality surrounding them. The only thing that really gives a strong indication of their need for help is the fact that many of them seek special help and confess to feelings of inadequacy.

In all three of these movements, the stimulus which induced movement seemed to be fear. This is not to say that fear is the driving force behind everything that man does, but it may give some real support to the idea that fear is a contingency factor around which humans move rather consistently.

In some cases, fear apparently plays some role. That is, although the original thesis that people are basically attempting to find closure remains the same, it also appears that the path to closure has to be considered in terms of fear contingencies. When the client reaches a point where he becomes overly apprehensive about making decisions and setting goals, he reaches a state of anxiety because he can no longer figure out alternatives by which he can find closure. Once in this state, his ability to function well is seriously reduced.

Computing Units of Emotional Stress (CUES)

Units of emotional stress quite typically reflect characteristics which define the three syndromes of movement. When reduced to simple descriptive terms, CUES look like this:

Dispirited Syndrome*

> Experiences loss of interest
> Is unable to concentrate
> Reflects low spirits
> Feels let down
> Has feelings of despair
> Feels depressed
> Feels life is hopeless
> Feels life is futile
> Withdraws from life experiences
> Talks of suicide
> Is self-accusatory
> Has feelings of remorse
> Feels rejected
> Has a low self-concept
> Experiences insomnia
> Experiences a loss of appetite
> Stays in bed excessively
> Shows marked nervousness
> Lacks energy
> Registers somatic complaints
> Experiences excessive fatigue
> Suffers from frequent colds

Rigid Syndrome

> Is precise
> Is meticulous
> Is methodical
> Is exacting
> Is overconscientious
> Is irreversible

---

*Note: All descriptive terms were taken from the Emotional Stress Checklist (See p. 147).

Is unyielding
Feels driven
Becomes obsessive
Worried over trifles
Has self-doubting tendencies
Feels inadequate
Becomes preoccupied with details
Seems to lack affection
Feels guilt laden
Is submissive
Becomes defensive
Projects blame
Seems insensitive to others
Is hypercritical
Is judgmental

Dramatic Syndrome
Is immature
Behaves seductively
Has shallow relationships
Seeks attention
Assumes roles
Appears warm and friendly
Seems flexible
Lacks identity
Has a flair for the dramatic
Is easily influenced by others
Imitates others
Shifts opinions when challenged
Appears helpless
Has flights of imagination
Experiences massive repression
Feels depersonalized
Overidentifies with others
Has limited intellectual interests
Lacks studious commitment
Spirits seem high

With each of these syndromes, the speed with which a person responds has to be considered as well as his total commitment to the contingency fear. If the person acts in haste, feels restless most of the time, shows little remorse for his acts, shows poor self-control, and rejects convention, then he is impulsive. This means that whatever he does will be done as a means of gaining immediate closure.

If he fears failure and constantly fears rejection by others, he is probably compulsive. Then, too, it should be remembered that any *Negative Inference,* even though not listed, will have to be treated as an emotional stress characteristic simply because negative inference always has been a typical indication of emotional stress (Ford and Urban, 1964).

Implementing a Press Technique

The press technique is one of the primary techniques in nexus psychotherapy. It is the means by which the client is placed in a position where he must contrast what he perceives in terms of what truly exists.

PERCEPTUAL CHIPPING. Perceptual chipping is a basic form of press which challenges the client's present interpretation of an experience by encouraging him to look at what he is doing in terms of the reality of the possible consequences. For example, when a client recently said the girl with whom he went to a movie would not go out with him again, the therapist responded with a perceptual chip by saying, "How would you know unless you asked? Have you asked?" His response was, "No!"

JUXTAPOSITION. Juxtaposition is a more sophisticated form of press which deals with comparing the reality of contrasting thoughts by bringing such thoughts together so that the client can reflect on what the contrasts mean. For example, in a recent therapy session, a male client said, "I just met a girl I'd like to date, but she won't go out with me." The therapist's perceptual chip was, "How would you know unless you asked?" He responded by saying, "I did ask, and she said she had a date." The therapist explored further by saying, "And what exactly was it she said?" He responded with, "She said she couldn't go because she already had a date," to which the therapist responded by using juxtaposition, "You said she wouldn't go; she said she couldn't go."

By placing these two statements in sharp contrast, the client immediately saw that she did not necessarily refuse to go out with him.

RECAPITULATION. Recapitulation is a facilitative technique by which the therapist takes the client back to contrasting statements. The purpose of recapitulation is to bring specific incongruencies into focus. It is a means by which the therapist moves the client back and forth between the world as he perceives it and the reality of that world in terms of what he must understand in order to get along and to feel good about himself.

Reality Testing

Ultimately, all of these steps are part of a press technique. Their purpose is to get the client to explore what he is saying in terms of the reality of the situation in which he finds himself. What the client says about his life and how poorly it has gone may be in conflict with the reality of the life he has. Naturally, he has the right to feel that things have gone poorly but only after he understands his potential to convert those failures into success. For example, in the illustration of juxtaposition, after the therapist had juxtaposed what the client had said against the reality of what the girl had said, the client felt that he could again approach the girl for a date. His response was, "Yeah, you're right." The therapist then responded, "At worst, what will happen if you ask her again?" He said, "I guess she could refuse."

It is extremely important to note that reality testing not only concerns itself with the reality of what exists but also with the reality of the consequences of what one is about to do. If a therapist wants his client to risk, then he must prepare him for such a risk.

The important thing about the press technique is that it permits the client to change his values through his own ability to reason from another point of view. There is never any value struggle between the therapist and his client; what the therapist says to a client can be treated or discarded. The key to introducing such a press involves placing what the person is perceiving against the reality of what exists, *i.e.* helping him to understand how to close the gap between what he sees and what prevails.

Through such press techniques as perceptual chipping and juxtaposition, the client becomes involved in the process of self-examination. Once this takes place, his attitudes about what has happened in the past usually change. With such a change in his thinking, he frequently finds alternatives which he never before realized were possible. As a result, he goes through a period of reality testing, trying out his new alternatives to see how well they work. If, in the process, he finds that he is relating better and feeling better about relationships, then his method of operation, *i.e.* his process of relating, begins to change and to become more compatible with his life goals.

The therapist continues to work with his client throughout this process of change, each time using the press technique to challenge any course of action which is in conflict with what seems to be in the client's best interests.

Some would ask, "Does the client have the right to choose?" The answer, of course, is that the client always makes the choice. The therapist simply introduces the challenge.

Working with clients in this fashion not only introduces flexibility of thought within the client, but also helps him to deal with failure. Failure cannot destroy a person who recognizes it for what it is—nothing more than an attitude. Yet, some will say that intervention by the therapist, which causes the client to recognize failure for what it is, superimposes the therapist's values and, thus, prevents the client from making a free choice. The truth of the matter is that people who are emotionally stressed are indecisive. What the therapist must attempt is to assist such a person to understand the reality of the decision he is about to make. He can do this by helping him to understand how he has made decisions in the past and how and why those decisions have failed. By doing this, he helps the client to understand that failure can never exist without his cooperation, unless, that is, the person who is making the decision withdraws from the responsibility of seeing it to its conclusion.

To carry out this sequence of steps, the therapist must have some basic understanding for implementing his method of therapy. Essentially, what this means is that he must have a basic language which explains his method of therapy well enough so that he can understand where he is and how to function within that setting. This is, to some extent, a vehicle language by which the process of therapy is executed.

For us, at least part of this language is included in the following basic concepts:

(1) *Desensitization.* For the client, desensitization is the process of examining highly resistant areas of stress and pairing his imaginary conceptualizations, which frequently produce his stress, against therapist-induced reality situations.

　It involves taking the client back to significant points of resistance and asking him what he has done in these situations to cause the stress that he experiences. When desensitization involves relationship problems, taking the client directly to the point of stress helps him to realize that much of what he experiences is a response to what he has done. It is at this point that he can explore the extent to which he is willing to change, to explore new alternatives and the consequences of such alternatives.

(2) *Confrontation.* Confrontation is the essence of self-examination. It places the client against himself in an exploration of his personal responsibility to those with whom he finds communication most difficult. In a sense, the therapist is helping him to examine what he is doing in his relationships to cause people to react as they do. If confrontation is successful, it frequently serves to counter the conditions which previously existed.

(3) *Counter Conditioning.* Counter Conditioning involves introducing a response inhibitor in the presence of an anxiety-evoking stimulus in an effort to weaken the bond be-

tween the condition, "anxiety," and the stimulus which evoked it. As an example, one might look at a client who seems predisposed to respond in terms of his feelings of abandonment. Because of his set patterns, he cannot see alternative courses of action. Through therapy, it is possible for him to weaken the bond between where he is in life and the set method by which he got there. The antagonist for change consists of a sequence of steps, the first of which calls for a reexamination of the client's major theme of thought and an examination of change potentials for those themes or patterns which cause the discomfort. Once his attitude changes, the client's coping strategies also change.

(4) *Coping.* Coping is the method by which individuals deal with life experiences. They are unlike defense mechanisms in that their primary function is not to defend a person against a hostile force but, rather, to serve as a means by which a person can grow, change, and transcend the position he is in. Coping Strategies are not necessarily "good" or "bad," they are simply organized ways of working with experiential situations. As strategies, they are learned and, therefore, can be unlearned, extinguished, or countered. If they are primary strategies, they concern themselves with methods by which the client deals with major areas of stress; if they are secondary, they are usually created to deal with the failure of primary strategies (Grebstein, 1969).

(5) *Stress.* Stress is a reaction to the situation which involves dealing with events that prove to be more than a person can handle by himself. The pattern by which the person deals with stress is his response pattern (Grebstein, 1969).

It sometimes helps a therapist to understand the source of stress and how the person is attempting to cope with it. Understanding this, the therapist can detect the areas in which the client is deficient and can assist him to assert himself in these areas by first asserting himself within the therapeutic relationship. The real advantage to relating in this way is that the client can reality test his new feelings and attitudes in the safety of a nonthreatening relationship with his therapist and can learn from this therapeutic relationship how he can generalize to the world around him.

FESTINGER'S DISSONANCE THEORY

The underlying basis for this approach rests with Festinger's Dissonance Theory (1957). It is Festinger's contention that maximum internal opinion change will result if the active participation in the defense of a position contrary to one's own belief is undertaken with minimum promise of reward.

There seems to be evidence in therapeutic practice that the amount of internalized change resulting from overcompliance in advocating a position contrary to the client's original position does, in fact, increase the client's potential for change.

Nexus psychotherapy incorporates a highly definitive self-examination which frequently encourages the client to accept a position he did not originally hold. The method by which this is executed is through perceptual chipping, getting a client to examine the incongruencies between his method of living and the goals he hopes to reach.

THE ROLE OF THE THERAPIST

The role of the therapist in this process is to serve as an agent of change. He serves as the catalyst between the client's world of misinterpretation and anticipation and the societal world of pragmatism and reality into which he grows.

As the therapist enters into helping relationships, he does so as both an artist and a scientist. He is sensitive and flexible in his personal relationship with his client, yet objective and pragmatic in the techniques he uses to help his client reach a better understanding of his total potential. His approach is not one of judgment but one of compassion. Yet his actions are tempered by the pragmatism of reality. If he is incapable of reality thinking, then his client will not have before him a person against whom he can test reality. Thus, he must be a person who has personally established a sound philosophy of life, for ultimately, he will serve as a model for his client. He models not because he wants to, but because he is selected as a model. It is his client's choice, not his.

When he is well trained, he becomes the center of his own system and the techniques he learns are delicately blended into that system. This makes what he does a normal and natural part of what he is. His relationships are not stultifying because he is not a "therapeutic-mechanic" who was indoctrinated into a school of thought. He is relaxed, flexible, and discreet in his relationships with others because he recognizes their need for understanding, and acceptance. Responding in this way, he becomes a model of objectivity, understanding, and acceptance. This is not what he pretends to be, but what he is.

The process by which therapists are trained must be designed to deal with both the need for accountability and the desire for effectiveness. One way in which nexus psychotherapy attempts to accept this challenge is by reducing the basic theoretical concepts introduced in this chapter to a method of science recognized as algorithm.

CHAPTER 3

SCHEMATIC ANALYSIS OF NEXUS PSYCHOTHERAPY THROUGH ALGORITHM

ONE OF THE CRITICAL ASPECTS of developing solutions to the myriad of difficulties presented to the therapist by his client is the analysis of fundamental problems. Typically, problem analysis is described as the process by which the difficulty is defined and all the basic information needed for problem solution is recognized.

In his text on interdisciplinary computer science, Walker (1972) has summarized the process of problem analysis as follows:

1. Development of a precise definition of the problem.
2. Identification of all significant subproblems.
3. Listing all required and available inputs (contributing factors).
4. Listing all desired outputs (solutions).

In therapeutic practice, problem analysis focuses on the interaction between the "becoming individual" and his environment, with special emphases given to his perceptions of the situation and his behavioral responses to it.

ALGORITHMIC SCHEMATIZATION

It is only after a problem has been appropriately analyzed that the therapist and client are in a position to develop a method for its solution. Because of its pragmatic basis, nexus psychotherapy seems to identify well with a method of computer science recognized as *algorithm,* "a procedure consisting of a set of *unambiguous* rules which specifies a *sequence* of operations that provides the *solution* to a problem in a *finite number* of steps (Walker, 1972)." In other words, an algorithm represents the problem solver's logic in arriving at the solution.

Unfortunately, however, it is not quite this simple when one attempts to present psychotherapeutic processes in algorithmic form. The major difficulty is encountered in refining one's communications into sets of "unambiguous rules." Computers, of course, require completely unambiguous steps to follow in the course of problem solution, and this criterion, though highly desirable in communicating the therapeutic process to therapists and other professionals, is difficult, if not impossible. Although the current evolutionary state of nexus psychotherapy has not achieved complete objectivity and scientific rigor, one of its major thrusts is toward this end.

Practically speaking, the algorithmic approach immediately enhances the system's level of objectivity and, of course, provides the format for ample opportunity for systematically increasing the longer-term scientific applications. Thus, the algorithmic approach to defining, understanding, predicting, and solving psychological and behavioral difficulties through nexus psychotherapy seems both desirable and expedient.

FLOWCHART LANGUAGE

To thoroughly understand how nexus psychotherapy and algorithm relate, it is necessary to have some basic knowledge of flowcharting, the language used in computer science and related fields. Basic to such an understanding is a knowledge of the following standard symbols.*

Terminal Box

Symbol:

The Terminal Box is an oval-shaped symbol which indicates the starting and stopping, or terminal, points in a flowchart.

---

*1. International Organization for Standardization (ISO) Recommendation R1028 Flowchart Symbols for Information Processing.

2. American National Standards Institute (ANSI) Standard Flowchart Symbols and their usage in Information Processing, ×3.5 — 1970.

3. International Business Machines (IBM) Usage beyond ISO and ANSI is the "Offpage Connector."

Processing Box

Symbol: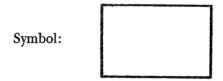

The Processing Box is a rectangular-shaped symbol which describes various processing functions or defined operations to be performed during the execution of the algorithm which cause change in the value, form, or location of information.

Annotation Box

Symbol: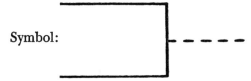

The Annotation Box is a rectangular-shaped symbol which has one end left open. It is connected to other flowchart boxes or flowlines by broken lines rather than flowlines because it does not contain executable steps of the algorithm. Annotation boxes are used for providing explanatory and/or descriptive information.

Decision Box

Symbol: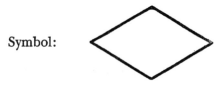

The Decision Box is a diamond-shaped symbol indicating a decision or switching-type operation that determines which of a number of alternative paths is to be followed. As a conditional branch, the processing of the information in the decision box determines which condition is satisfied, and hence which alternative branch is to be taken in the sequence.

Out-Connector

Symbol:

An Out-Connector is a circle that has a flowline pointing toward it. It indicates that flow is to exit at this point and will resume in the part of the flowchart indicated by the reference number in the circle. As such, the out-connector becomes an unconditional branch.

In-Connector

Symbol: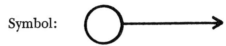

An In-Connector is a circle that has a flowline leading from it which points to another flowline or flowchart box. Hence, it is a point in the flowchart where flow is to resume. It is thus used as a branch point by out-connectors elsewhere in the flowchart.

Flowline

Symbol: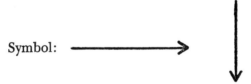

Flowlines are straight lines with attached arrowheads. Flowchart symbols are connected to each other by flowlines used to indicate the sequence in which the steps of the algorithm are to be executed.

Offpage Connector

Symbol:

Offpage Connectors are five-sided, "house-shaped," special IBM symbols used to indicate entry to or exit from a page (as indicated by the reference inside it), depending on the direction of the connecting flowlines.

Flowchart Box Numbers

Example:  16

Each flowchart box, with the exception of the annotation box, has an identifying number just above it on the righthand side. These numbers are convenient reference indexes permitting us to refer to specific boxes and/or their process functions by simply citing their respective flowchart box numbers.

LEARNING IN NEXUS THEORY

We are now prepared to approach the fundamental principles of nexus psychotherapy with the aid of algorithmic schematization. Hill (1963) has attested that the systematic interpretation of the learning process has an important place both in the science of psychology as well as in the application of psychology to education. While retaining the essence of his thought but modifying the scene from academia to psychotherapy, let us begin by graphically illustrating the nexus view of learning.

The definitions for "learning" and "behavior" will be recalled from Chapter 2,

Learning: The process of utilizing experiences in ways which provide alternatives which were not possible before the experiences occurred. Learning is the birth of a new response possibility.

Behavior: Random or organized patterns of responding to experiences—typical ways of responding.

Figure 1 depicts a more detailed and comprehensive overview of this learning/change process

Initially, process boxes 1 and 2 depict the simultaneous input influences from both the humanistic and behavioristic perspectives, respectively.

On the humanistic side, we have the biological organism operating in and upon his environment. Here, man is considered an

THE LEARNING PROCESS

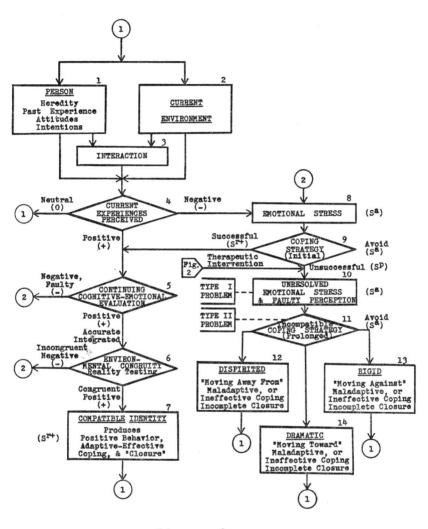

Figure 1

independent variable to the extent that he is making decisions independently, *i.e.* making decisions based on the unique way these forces come together and are internalized. This ongoing operation is generated from his relativistic vantage point which is based on his previous experience as well as his specific interpretations of the present situation. This, of course, includes his attitudes, intentions, values, assignments of meaning, and cognitive interpretations of reality. Here, we are dealing with the data of human experience; that is, the "reality" of the present situation as it is evaluated against the backdrop of previous experience and "sized-up" within the individual's contemporary dynamic frame of reference. Responses are altered depending upon perceptions. Learning is in process.

Concomitantly, learning can also be traced to environmental forces and factors. Various objective stimuli constantly impinge upon the person from without and influence/elicit behavioral responses. Here, man is considered a dependent variable to the extent that he accepts models or permits external forces to shape his life. A tremendous advantage of the behavioral perspective is that both the stimuli and the responses are identified, observed, quantified, and objectively recorded. Specific sequences of behavior can thus be linked to external schedules of reinforcement, punishment, and extinction to document environmental influences in the learning process. Responses are altered depending on the environmental contingencies. Learning is in process.

An obvious question which seems to arise at this point is, "Which of the above models—humanism or behaviorism—best exemplifies learning?" The answer of a nexus therapist would be, "Neither one is best, but both are good, so I use them in combination." Although fundamentally different in approach, humanism and behaviorism need not be mutually exclusive. Since they are both valuable mediums for understanding learning, nexus psychotherapy proposes a combination phenomenological/environmental "interaction" framework where both theoretical approaches contribute (*see* process box 3) toward a more comprehensive and natural therapeutic understanding of the total person in his environmental situation. Learning is, thus, intimately tied to stimulus-response (s-r) connections, but is frequently mediated by the purposing organism's perceptions of the situation. The model then is an s-O-r (stimulus-Organism-response) paradigm, without exclusive emphasis being placed on any single element.

All the elements are contributory; all are important; all are considered. Consequently, both theoretical orientations are helpful in providing primary input variables of major consequence in initial learning as well as therapeutic remediation (new learning).

In this interaction process (which, incidentally, is sometimes dominated by one of the two variables), all experience takes place. Experience is constantly subject to evaluation, although the process is often without conscious effort or thought. Moreover, the evaluative process can be subjective, objective, or in mixed combinations. If, for example, the current experience (as depicted in decision box 4) is initially perceived as being relatively neutral (of no particular influence either positive or negative), the process effects no change contingencies, and flow is returned to in-connector 1 to initiate a new cycle. If, however, the experience is initially given a positive value, the flow continues toward decision box 5 for further cognitive-affective evaluation. If, upon evaluation, the initial value is judged to be faulty or in error, flow is shifted to in-connector 2 where the incongruency produces stress (process box 8). Conversely, if the cognitive-affective decision is positive, the organism attempts to integrate the experience into its reproducible response repertoire and conceptualized self-identity.

As the individual integrates the experience and attempts to reproduce it, it undergoes the reality testing depicted in decision box 6. In the actual testing here (as opposed to the reflective testing in decision box 5), the experience may not be reproducible, or upon reiteration, may be judged negatively. This type of incongruency once again would shift the flow to in-connector 2 and resultant stress. On the other hand, if the experience at box 6 is judged to be positive, it can be incorporated into the individual's compatible positive self-identity as is shown in process box 7.

If, at any choice point, the flow is transferred to process box 8 where emotional stress is encountered, we once again witness dual potential consequences emerging from the coping strategies enlisted to deal with the stress. If the strategy is successful in eliminating the incongruency, thus reducing or eliminating the stress, this experience is positively reinforced and the flow returns to the "compatible identity" course for further evaluation and integration when the flow reaches process box 7.

Compatible identity, in process box 7, represents the results of healthy learning processes as mediated by positive and successful experiences. This represents the route primarily travelled in the acquisition of good mental health and adaptive behavior that is effective in coping with one's experiences. This resolution of an experience by bringing it into the individual's total system of functioning constitutes "closure." Closure, then, serves as a vital link in the individual's means to identity.

If, however, the initial coping strategies evolving at decision box 9 are unsuccessful in alleviating the stress which prompted their need for existence, a Type I problem develops. That is, the individual is caught in a vicious cycle of unresolved stress. Additional stress, due to the failure of the coping strategy, is compounded along with the initial stress. In this situation, the individual's attitudes, values, interest patterns, self-identity concepts, and feelings begin to change. In the midst of this perceptual distortion, the individual can become destructively fixated within channels of confusion, conflict, negative self-appraisal, and frustration. In essence, he no longer maintains full recognition of who he is and where he wants to go, much less how to successfully negotiate the journey. These faulty perceptions (Type I problem) form the principal foundation upon which many of the neuroses and psychoses are built.

Chronic Type I problems almost invariably lead to further cognitive ineffectiveness, emotional frustration, faulty intentions, unrealistic fantasizing, and deficient attempts at solution. Prolonged deficient and incompatible coping patterns evolve into a faulty method of operation syndrome, depicted as a Type II problem in decision box 11. Basically, there are three typical, Type II faulty method of operation response syndromes. These are the (1) *Dispirited,* (2) the *Rigid,* and (3) the *Dramatic* as were described in Chapter 2 and here are shown in process boxes 12, 13, and 14, respectively.

Notice in Figure 1 that each experience can follow a number of alternate flow routes and, with the exception of rare neutral events, each one eventually influences what is learned and the way in which it is learned. What is learned and the way that it is learned in turn determine one's attitudes, knowledge, perceptions, and behavioral responses both with regard to the person and salient aspects of his environment.

If this is a pragmatic and heuristic theory of learning (as nexus therapists we believe it is), then it not only provides explanations to aid our understanding of etiological dynamics, but also gives us a solid theoretical basis for therapeutic intervention modalities. Intervention procedures, as will be inserted at the flowpoint indicated by the offpage connector labeled "Figure 2," will be discussed in the next two sections.

NEXUS THERAPY FOR TYPE I PROBLEMS
Introduction to Therapy

The work of nexus psychotherapy begins, quite appropriately, with the individual's feelings, beliefs, and perceptions of his problem situation. Many of these conceptualizations are, as previously outlined, faulty. This is principally due to the unresolved emotional stress surrounding unsuccessful initial coping strategies. This stress contributes to the production of negative cognitive and affective changes which are described as Type I problems.

Thus, our algorithmic schematization of nexus therapy begins with the therapeutic process that deals with personal ineffectiveness based on these faulty perceptions. For clarity, however, preliminary client and therapist decisions and interaction, prefacing the therapeutic intervention, initiate the flowchart depicting nexus therapy for Type I problems shown in Figure 2.

As indicated by the offpage connector labeled "Figure 1," this part of our process intervenes into the individual's flow of faulty or negative learning (as shown in Fig. 1 by the offpage reference for Fig. 2) with the following therapeutic approach. The nexus approach first centers on attitudes observable through topical patterns reflected in the client-therapist interaction. Then, some attitude-changing techniques are encountered.

First, of course, the initial willingness of the individual to participate in self-exploration and change through the therapeutic

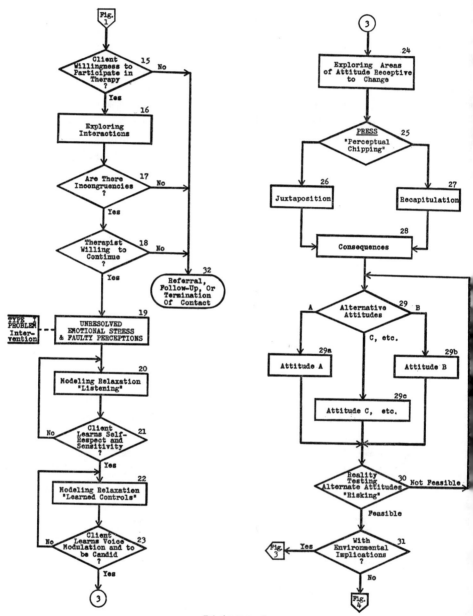

Figure 2

process is investigated (see decision box 15). If the individual is unwilling or for some reason cannot participate in therapy, the case is either terminated or appropriate follow-up and/or referral is made. When therapy is initiated, the process of exploring interactions within the client's phenomenological frame of reference (process box 16) offers the therapist initial understanding of the client's perceived world. As the therapist is attaining insight into the attitudes, interests, values, and desires of his client, he also is engaging in the cognitive process of cataloging incongruencies within his perceptions and activities.

At this point, the therapist has two decisions to make. First, does the client manifest a Type I problem, i.e. are there incongruencies within his perceptual functioning and attitudinal approach to "reality?" Actually, the probability of encountering no substantial incongruencies within the client's interactions is slight. However, if this is the case, flow shifts to terminal box 32 for referral, follow-up, or termination. More typically, incongruencies are noted and, as such, they contribute toward precipitating the therapist's second determination. This professional decision (shown in box 18) involves the therapist's willingness to continue the therapeutic relationship based on two things: (1) his professional competency within the manifest problem area(s) and (2) the compatibility of his personal and professional ethics/standards with those expressed by the would-be client. Again, if the decision is in the negative, flow shifts to terminal box 32. More frequently, however, the decision will be to continue the therapeutic process.

It is important to keep two things in mind as we progress through the algorithmic flowcharts of nexus therapy. First, in actual practice, the techniques are not always as discrete as they are depicted. For example, the therapist will frequently find himself involved in multiple techniques simultaneously. However, the discrete schematization is to emphasize direction, alternatives, and clarity of process within each specific technique. Second, the flow is not strictly restricted to the depicted sequence, nor does it necessarily include all the steps we cover in the schematization. In other words, the flowcharts are meant to represent comprehensive general models from which idiosyncratic composites evolve during individual therapy cases. Lest the reader become overly dubious following these qualifications, we hasten to add that most of the steps will be present, and they will follow a sequence similar to that depicted.

At this juncture, we now are ready to begin exploring nexus techniques and processes designed to achieve the resolution of emotional stress and the correcting of faulty perceptual functioning (*see* process box 19).

Type I Problem Intervention

As in most therapies, nexus therapy begins with the therapist's commitment to the client This commitment is indicated by the therapist's careful attention to what his client is saying, both explicitly and implicitly. Careful listening provides the means by which the therapist develops an awareness of the client's perceptions and incongruencies. Even more important, however, is the fact that careful listening by the therapist provides the client with two other therapeutically vital phenomena. The first of these is a "model of relaxation," as shown in process box 20. The client experiences an encounter with another person who can relax to the point of concentrating his listening attention. In other words, the therapist becomes a model of emotional and physical relaxation before the client. In this environment of stability where attention is focused on understanding the client's feelings, thoughts, and problems, an opportunity for the second therapeutic phenomenon is created. That is, the client typically responds to the sensitivity and respect given him by the therapist by internalizing these factors. Thus, decision box 21 depicts the change in terms of whether or not the client is learning self-respect and sensitivity from his model through the therapeutic interaction. To the extent that these characteristics are modeled and attained, parallel relaxation should also be acquired.

Relaxation also is modeled by the therapist through what we term "learned controls" (process box 22). These include voice modulation and the overall composure of the therapist. In this way, the qualities of responsibility and maturity are exemplified before the client. As learned controls are modeled, the client begins to understand that a less emotionally upsetting and more constructive approach can be implemented toward the solution of his problems and, concomitantly, the reduction of his experienced anxiety. In the process, he also begins to temper his own voice quality with calmness and relaxation. That is, he begins to speak more slowly, softly, and with a calmness reflecting greater self-confidence. Moreover, the client learns to become more candid, since the experienced anxiety reduction serves to negatively reinforce the therapeutic process of problem exploration (decision box 23).

Through the therapeutic use of empathic listening and learned controls, the client experiences an atmosphere of respect, caring, concern, and understanding regarding his feelings and perceived difficulties. Moreover, despite the emotionally volatile content of the sessions, he experiences a certain calmness, relaxation, and control over affective material through his therapist-model. As he himself begins to experience this lessening of tension, a new hope evolves for changing that which he may have considered an impossible dilemma. These techniques simultaneously serve to help the client to increase his self-confidence, self-respect, objectivity regarding his situation, and openness of problem discussion. Once these characteristics begin to emerge, the client is ready to engage in exploratory interaction with the therapist with respect to specific problem areas he now wishes to change (process box 24).

It is, of course, the client who ultimately must comprehend what it is about himself that is hindering the accomplishment of his goals and, therefore, should be changed. Thus, the therapist's primary function is to act as a catalyst throughout the exploration. Such catalytic action is facilitated by the press technique which utilizes as its primary contingency a tactic recognized as "perceptual chipping," constantly challenging the faulty perception of a stressed person. One form of the press technique is juxtaposition. Juxtapositioning involves tactfully confronting the client with the incongruencies between his faulty perceptual conclusions (his personal idiosyncratic phenomenal "reality") and more objective alternative conclusions (external "reality"). Decision box 25 depicts this process as offering two basic types of press technique: juxtaposition and recapitulation. The therapist uses these press techniques as circumstances and opportunities in the session warrant.

Juxtaposition (depicted in process box 26) is always preceded by perceptual chipping which is nothing more than challenging the client's present course of action. Juxtaposition is one specific way in which the challenge is made. It requires that the therapist pose two or more of the client's conflicting statements, feelings, and/or ideas in parallel position, thus challenging the client to bring these contrasting statements into some form of reality. The therapeutic task, of course, is to focus the client on the discordance between his expressed desires and the faulty attitudinal processes he has developed while attempting to gain his objectives.

Recapitulation (depicted in process box 27) as a press technique involves taking the client back to previously contrasting statements. The purpose of recapitulation is to invoke the client's recall of formerly expressed material which is incongruent with the achievement of past, present, or future goals.

Obviously, the primary function of the press technique and, therefore, of perceptual chipping is to actively involve the client in the process of self-examination. He is challenged to examine his faulty perceptions in the light of conflicting evidence that he himself has directly or indirectly expressed. Moreover, he is challenged to evaluate both the previous, as well as probable continuing, consequences of his perceptions, attitudes and, in general, his phenomenological frame of reference (process box 28). He is very subtly and effectively placed in a position where he must admit that, at least in part, he had an active role in producing many of the undesirable results in his experience. Likewise, if one is at least partially responsible for his dilemmas, then his understanding of how he can organize his life more realistically and, thus, assure greater responsibility, controls the outcome of the course of action he takes, just as his lack of reality governed his life process before therapy.

Ultimately, the work of nexus therapy is to bridge the relationship between the objective reality existing outside the mind and the individual's thought of it. Nexus psychotherapy for Type I problems simply involves the "unveiling" of those perceptual distortions which cause faulty interpretations of experiences.

During this unveiling and exploration of dysfunctional perceptual processes, the client typically gives many indications of understanding some of the underlying factors of his dilemma. However, despite these newly acquired insights, most clients do not automatically make the desired perceptual shift to more healthy approaches. Therefore, accompanying such moments of insight, it is usually advisable for the therapist to encourage his client to conceive several potentially feasible alternative attitudes and their possible consequences (decision box 29). Although our schematic illustrates three potential alternative attitudes (choice points A, B, and C), the actual number of options considered is, of course, relative.

When the client, in interaction with the therapist, develops a potentially feasible alternative and has cognitively considered the probable results of implementing it, it is time for him to "try it out." This empirical process of reality testing (decision box 30) simply involves risking the proposed perceptual change and noting its effects. Although it may appear obvious to the reader that such a perceptual shift involves concomitant behavioral expression (which we will discuss later), we now are primarily concerned with attitude (perceptual) change. The accompanying behavioral changes, at this point, are not specifically formulated. They are, rather, allowed to "spontaneously" evolve from the "natural" implementation of the change in attitude.

It would appear that at least three types of results could occur in the reality testing of attitude/perceptual changes. First, the encountered reactions could document negative or counter-productive consequences. In this case, the flow returns to decision box 29 to resume formulation of new perceptual options. Second, if the attitude being tested is in itself feasibly compatible with the reality of the situation, but some environmental obstacles impede full implementation of the change (decision box 31), flow is shifted to a subalgorithm designed to deal with environmental blocks *(see* offpage connector for Fig. 3). Third, if a proposed alternative proves to be compatible with reality and encounters no environmental obstacles, we are ready to link the Type I therapeutic intervention modality to the Type II intervention strategies *(see* offpage connector for Fig. 4). Type II intervention focuses on changing faulty methods of operation, in addition to the nexus process for changing faulty perceptual processes through Type I operations. Before discussing the nexus combination of Type I and II intervention strategies, let us review the algorithmic schemata for dealing with the occurrence of environmental obstacles.

Environmental Factors

If, during the reality testing of alternative attitudes (or at other therapy junctures), it becomes apparent that environmental factors may be impeding therapeutic progress, the flow is shifted to the offpage connector labeled "Figure 3," and, consequently, to process box 33 which initiates the therapeutic flow depicted in Figure 3.

Logically, when environmental impedances to therapeutic progress are encountered, the first consideration should involve the exploration of possible environmental changes toward effecting a remediation of the impasse. The more feasible of these potential alternatives are then segregated for formal evaluation (decision box 34). Some of these environmental changes will involve only simple manipulation of the client's surroundings, as are shown in alternatives A and C. However, other alternatives chosen for empirical testing may involve more complex interventions including a combination of behavioral changes in conjunction with the environmental manipulation (as depicted in alternative B).

These suggested alternatives must, of course, be subjected to the test of their respective consequences as they are implemented. This reality testing, with three initial relative evaluation outcomes, is displayed in decision box 35. If the alternative in question is proven unsatisfactory, flow is returned to decision box 34 for consideration of other potential alternatives. If, on the other hand, the alternative proves to be complete and effective, flow is shifted to the offpage connector labeled "Figure 4" for continua-

DEALING WITH ENVIRONMENTAL BLOCKS

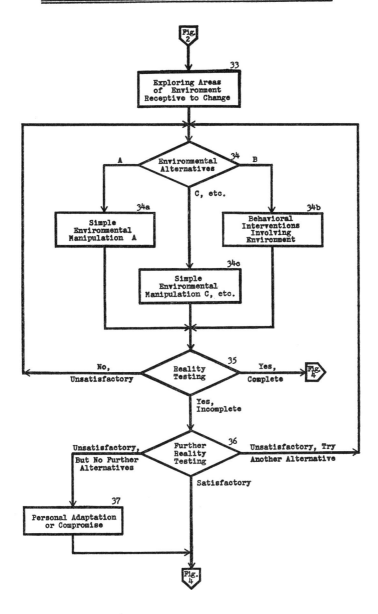

Figure 3

tion of the nexus approach to Type II problems. If, as a third possible outcome, the alternative seems to be providing some satisfactory but inconclusive results, flow is continued to decision box 36 for additional reality testing. This further reality testing likewise involves three possible outcome routes. First, the additional empirical testing may prove the alternative to be unsatisfactory after all, whereupon the flow returns to decision box 34 to repeat the process. Second, even though the alternative may be shown to be unsatisfactory, all competing alternatives may be unobtainable or have been eliminated as being even less satisfactory. In this case, when there may be no further environmental recourse, therapy is directed toward the development of an acceptable personal adaptation compromise with the situation. Third, when the additional reality testing evidence indicates the alternative to be satisfactory, flow is shifted directly to the offpage connector labeled "Figure 4" and into the final major phase of nexus therapy which is designed to deal with Type II problems.

NEXUS THERAPY FOR TYPE II PROBLEMS

As we have just seen, Type I problem therapy involves the changing of maladaptive and faulty attitudes through the therapeutic facilitation of insight and subsequent reality testing. Despite the fact that attitudinal and perceptual changes frequently occur in Type I nexus therapy, this does not, in itself, guarantee successful generalization of the client's newfound insights to his habitual faulty coping strategies (Type II problem). Regarding this necessary induction of accurate insight throughout the individual's behavioral processes, Bigge (1964) stated:

Truth, relativistically defined, "is that quality of an insight which enables its possessor to design behavior which is successful in that it achieves what it is designed to achieve" [Bayles, 1960]. Insights derive from a person's best interpretations of what comes to him; they may be deeply discerning or they may not. They may serve as dependable guides for action or they may prove ruinous.

Insights are to be considered, not as literal descriptions of objective physical-social situations, but as interpretations of one's perceived environment on the basis of what subsequent action can be designed. Although insights are not physicalistic descriptions of objects or processes, they necessarily take account of the physical environment. Their usability depends in part on how well this is done. . . .An insight is usable to a learner only if he can "fit it in."

Hence, once again the humanistic-behavioristic link provided by nexus therapy manifests its value in offering therapeutic continuity. Type I perceptual/attitudinal shifts are joined together with concomitant behavioral strategies designed to enhance the client's coping effectiveness. This latter factor, of course, involves nexus intervention into Type II problems, *i.e.* the changing of faulty methods of operation. Type II nexus intervention assists the client in examining the incongruencies between his objectives and the behavioral processes he uses in his attempts to reach those objectives.

Type II Problem Intervention

Once the perceptual difficulties are well understood by both client and therapist, alternative attitudinal approaches have been reality tested, and environmental blocks eliminated, it is time for the nexus therapist to initiate therapeutic intervention designed to combat incompatible coping strategies (as first depicted in box 11 of Fig. 1). The algorithmic schematization of Type II problem intervention is depicted in Figure 4.

As indicated by the initial offpage connector, this part of the Nexus process continues from the therapeutic procedures depicted in Figures 2 and 3. Type II problem intervention begins with an exploration of faulty methods of operation (coping strategies) and hopefully concludes (if therapy is successful) with closure through the implementation of more appropriate response modes.

Although process box 38 discretely depicts the exploration of faulty response patterns, the process for the therapist actually has been an ongoing one from the very initiation of therapy. However, formal interactive exploration is deliberately reserved until this point in the client's progress. This is because the preliminary perceptual work more pragmatically precedes the client's effective

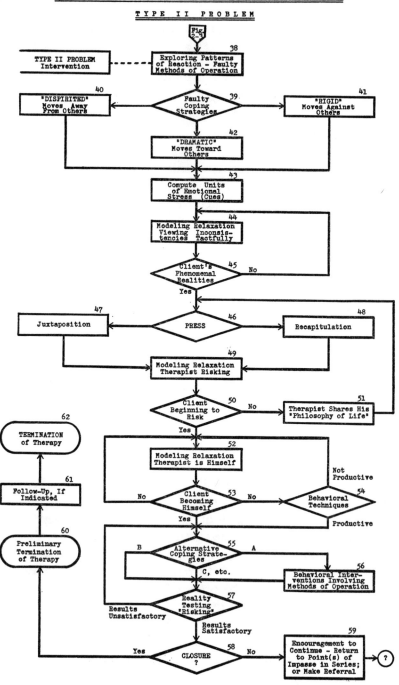

Figure 4.

participation in altering his habitual response patterns.

As previously discussed, prolonged deficient and incompatible coping strategies evolve into three basic Type II faulty method of operation syndromes *(see* decision box 39). These syndromes are depicted in process boxes 40 through 42 and are described as (1) Dispirited, (2) Rigid, and (3) Dramatic, respectively (if necessary, refer back to Chap. 2 for a thorough review).

Since by this time the therapist has a fairly clear conception of the client's behavioral themes and primary coping strategies, the therapeutic task is to clarify them in the client's understanding and to remediate them. If, for example, the client's principal movements involve the Dispirited syndrome (process box 40), the therapeutic emphasis would be concentrated upon alleviating major symptoms such as those listed in Table I. Tables II and III

TABLE I
NEXUS THERAPY WITH DISPIRITED CLIENTS

Response Symptomatology	*Corresponding Therapeutic Task*
1. Moves Away From Others	1. Induce & Reinforce Involvement
2. Lethargic, Apathetic	2. Incorporate Goal Setting and Striving
3. Fears Failure, Avoids Decision	3. Structure Graduated Risking
4. Projects Blame, Feels Victimized	4. Assumption of Appropriate Responsibility
5. Dwells on Past	5. Instill Contemporary and Future Orientation
6. Feels Useless	6. Initiate and Reinforce Constructive Activity

TABLE II
NEXUS THERAPY WITH RIGID CLIENTS

Response Symptomatology	*Corresponding Therapeutic Task*
1. Moves Against Others	1. Induce and Reinforce Cooperation
2. Meticulous, Perfectionistic	2. Relaxation of Compulsivity
3. Fears Failure and Rejection	3. Acceptance of Limitations
4. Attacks, Criticizes Others	4. Acceptance of Self and Others
5. Projects Structure onto Others	5. Avoidance of Intrusion
6. Desires Complete Control	6. Tolerance for Ambiguity

TABLE III
NEXUS THERAPY WITH DRAMATIC CLIENTS

Response Symptomatology	*Corresponding Therapeutic Task*
1. Moves Toward Others	1. Induce and Reinforce Constructive Independence
2. Role Playing — Seductiveness	2. Reinforce Genuineness and Encourage Being True to Oneself
3. Shallowness in Relationships	3. Induce and Reinforce Deeper Involvement
4. Feels Inadequate	4. Structure Successful Risking

show the therapeutic emphases for the Rigid (process box 41) and the Dramatic (process box 42) syndromes, respectively.

Let us now proceed to outline the general nexus Type II process, which incorporates the above specific therapeutic emphases, as warranted. As an aid both to the therapist and the client, units of emotional stress are computed (process box 43) using the Emotional Stress Checklist (ESC). For obvious research purposes, the authors recommend pre- and post-therapy administrations of the ESC in addition to this midtherapy evaluation. The midtherapy ESC results provide an index of progress in therapy and also identify areas needing continued special attention.

Process box 44 emphasizes the continuing need for modeling relaxation by tactfully and rationally discussing the apparent inconsistencies between that which the client perceives and the reality of what exists. This is done as a foundation for the perceptual chipping which follows, and serves to bring the client's perceptions of his faulty method of operation into a form closer to reality (decision box 45) where it (the Type II problem) can be therapeutically challenged. That is, the client begins to see the flaws in his modus operandi. The second major facet of the therapeutic process, wherein the faulty behavioral patterns can be altered, is now facilitated through the use of the press technique (decision box 46). In this process, the incongruencies between the client's perception of an experience and the reality of that experience can be examined and changed. Through perceptual chipping, recapitulation, and juxtaposition, the reality of these conflicting phenomena are brought together so the client can reflect on what the incongruencies mean. Once again, the therapist uses the twin techniques of juxtaposition (process box 47) and recapitulation (process box 48) to confront the client with his apparent inconsistencies. These press techniques help the client to explore the incongruencies between what he perceives and the reality of what exists. This is a process which assists the client to understand his own role in the precipitation of his problems. In addition, it will be noted in process box 49 that, while such confrontation is in process, the therapist becomes a model of risking before the client. That is, because he cares for the client's welfare, he exposes himself to the client's critical evaluation of the relationship by assuming the role of a reality-based confronter. In actuality, however, the relationship seldom suffers as a result of such therapeutic confrontation. In fact, when the therapist uses the press technique skillfully, the relationship typically is enhanced. Moreover, because the client experiences such encounters where the respected therapist risks himself to facilitate therapeutic change, he frequently begins to commit himself to making a response change and risking the consequences involved in such reality testing (decision box 50). The client thus turns to the therapist for a model of risking because he typically has no other frame of reference from which to draw.

Risking is, of course, paramount to successful living and good mental health. Thus, the constricted client has reached a point where he must risk in order to grow. If, during the pressing and modeling exercises of this period of therapy, the client remains unwilling to risk new approaches, the therapist explicitly shares his own "philosophy of life" and the necessity for risking (process box 51). As he does this, he continues to perceptually chip in an effort to keep his client from reverting back to previous methods which did not work. Conversely, if the client is beginning to explore personal risking, the therapeutic process proceeds with additional modeling of relaxation.

Although the nexus therapist consistently presents himself in a genuine manner, at this particular point more emphasis is centered upon this facet of therapy (process box 52). The client's ability to become his own person depends, to a great extent, on the therapist's approach. When the therapist is completely himself in the interaction, the client is more likely to recognize that he can become completely himself (decision box 53). If the client is failing to establish his own personal identity, flow is channeled to decision box 54 where a choice of behavioral and/or cognitive techniques is made to overcome the obstacles impeding such progress. Some example techniques might include conditioning, counterconditioning, desensitization, more modeling of relaxation and constructive teaching.

When the client reaches a point where he can risk being himself and has experienced moderate success in this newfound approach, the final focus of nexus therapy is imminent. This phase involves the formulation of alternative coping strategies to supplant his faulty response patterns (decision box 55). By this time, the client's Type II problem should be as clear to him as it is to the therapist. Thus, alternative strategies may be either mutually contemplated and mapped out, or the client simply may decide that he now knows what he needs to do. In either case, the specific alternative strategies are shown as flowlines A, B and C emanating from decision box 55. While B and C depict simple response shifts, in general contexts, flowline A depicts the route taken by more complex alternatives requiring programmed behavioral intervention (process box 56). In these instances, the particular response alternative may be either complex or not yet under the stimulus control of the problem situation for the client. For such cases, specific behavioral/environmental interventions are programmed to assist the client in implementing and developing the desired strategy.

Once again, of course, the new response must prove to be feasible in application. As with all other therapeutic alterations, the experimental coping pattern must be tested in the crucible of reality. When the trial coping strategy is inadequate, the consequences typically will prove to be less than satisfactory or counterproductive and, as such, induce stress through potential failure. However, with the therapist's assistance, such faulty alternatives are rejected and replacement alternatives are reality tested until success is achieved. The therapeutic difference in nexus therapy is that faulty attitudes and coping strategies are not permitted to become further entrenched. Instead, they are countered and replaced on the pragmatic basis of reality tests (decision box 57). Once successful strategies are found and implemented, the client discovers that he is relating better and feeling better about his relationships. These positive consequences powerfully reinforce the new response pattern, thus maintaining and strengthening it. In other words, the client has learned, through the nexus process, how to obtain feedback from others that is more compatible with his life goals. In effect, he achieves closure, the successful resolution of an experience (decision box 58). This resolution of an experience, by bringing it into the individual's total system of functioning, serves as a vital link in the individual's means to identity.

If, as occurs only rarely, the client is unable to formulate and implement successful coping strategies and, thus, is unable to achieve closure, flow is shifted to process box 59. Here, an in-depth evaluation of the difficulty, including encouragement to continue therapy at the point of impasse, is executed. Or, if either party believes the interaction would not be of further benefit, an appropriate referral is made.

More typically, however, when satisfactory resolution of the difficulties has resulted in therapeutic closure, flow shifts to terminal box 60 for preliminary termination of therapy with appropriate follow-up (process box 61), or simply to unconditional termination (terminal box 62).

CHAPTER 4

NEXUS PSYCHOTHERAPY AS AN ART
OF RELATING

THERE HAS LONG BEEN a mystique about counseling and psychotherapy which seems to emerge as much from the difficulty involved in defining these terms as it does from the fact that people are less interested in the science of relating than in the practice. It is this very same difficulty which makes it almost impossible to reduce counseling methodology to the empirical test of effectiveness demanded by Hans Eysenck (1952) so many years ago. Although his attack on the efficacy of counseling and psychotherapy stimulated some research in this area (Cartwright, 1960; Patterson, 1964; Rogers, 1961; Malan, 1973; and Diloreto, 1971), there are still serious questions about its value (Bixler, 1963; Eysenck, 1964; Levitt, 1957; Sloane et al., 1975).

Relatively speaking, however, Nexus Psychotherapy seems to be both an art and a science As an art, it is a rather loosely structured variable which depends to a great extent upon the personality of the therapist. As a science, it is a rather tightly structured constant which depends to a great extent on the skills of the therapist. The challenge of the therapist is to blend these qualities together in his attempt to serve as the catalyst by which his client develops a greater awareness of reality and a more intensified philosophy of life. Ultimately, it is this cognitive change which encourages his client to risk participating in experiences he has never before had.

Naturally, for each therapist the uniqueness of his approach is reflected in the process by which he brings his subjectivity for people into play with his objectivity about people. This means that in practice there can only be one Freudian psychoanalyst, one Rogerian client-centered therapist, and one Glasserian Reality therapist. While it is true that many professional therapists have styled themselves after these highly creative men, it is also true that the unique feelings such therapists have about themselves and their clients is the basis for the art by which they differ. It is the reality by which these differences exist that dictates the idea that whatever people feel has some impact on how they respond. It also became apparent that each respondent has some concern for his own well-being. What this means in practice is that people spend a good deal of time attempting to understand how they relate to the world around them. Their directions are encouraged by what brings the greatest pleasure or avoids the greatest pain (Freud, 1919). Logically speaking, this may also mean that, typically, people seek security or avoid fear (Urban and Ford, 1964).

Recognizing this as a basis from which new understandings can emerge, it can be assumed that one learns by having experiences but that what one learns is not necessarily a reflection of what one has experienced. Because a person is capable of personal interpretations; it must be assumed that the interpretation placed upon any given experience will have much to do with the physiological makeup of the person having the experience and his ability to handle that experience.

THE CASE OF MAT

One case which illustrates this quite vividly is the case of Mat. When Mat first requested nexus therapy he was thirty-six years old and had been under psychiatric care for sixteen of those years. During those sixteen years, he had attempted suicide five times and had threatened suicide over a dozen times. He was a veritable entourage of gloom, despair, and remorse. His shirts, pants, socks, and shoes all seemed remarkably alike in color—a rather dismal olive drab. The small gold-rimmed glasses he wore dropped to the end of his nose with remarkable ease and then stuck there like hot tar on a clean car. His features were flat, his lips thick, and his hair disheveled. There was nothing really distinctive about Mat except his indistinctiveness.

Only recently he had married and his marriage compounded his emotional problems. His wife was an extension of his depression. Everything he felt and did seemed to become manifest in her reactions. It was almost like *folie à deux* where two people who are closely related mutually share delusions. Yet there was always a touch of *la maladie du doute,* the illness of doubt. He once said of his wife, "I'm not sure I can trust her. She's a lot like my mother. Some of the bad feelings I have toward her are the same as those I have toward my mother. . ."

He was referring to the idea that he thought his mother had abandoned him for his sister when he was quite young.* Up to that time, she had dressed him like a little girl and was overly attentive to him. Although his relationship with little boys was not enhanced by such a motherly display, it did make him feel that he was unloved. He referred to this period as the happiest period in his life. When asked what happiness was he said, "Well I don't really know; it was having somebody to talk to and to be with. It was being with my mother."

After his sister was born, however, his mother no longer dressed him like a little girl, and he suddenly felt abandoned, alone, and rejected. Actually, it was from this point on that he started to doubt his relationship with his mother. This was probably as much because he did not know how to react to abandonment as because of the abandonment itself.

In a sense, his experience and the way he reacted to that experience were diametrically opposed; when he needed his mother's love the most, he responded to her in hateful ways. His responding pattern was based primarily on his youth, i.e. the fact that he was only five years old at the time his sister was born and was unable to deal with the loss of his mother's undivided attention. Not understanding his mother's new responsibilities, Mat feared the relationship had changed. In reality, his mother did

---

*Interestingly enough, Baer (1962) found that withholding positive reinforcers, such as is true in Mat's case with his loss of positive attention by his mother, causes greater dependency, especially in children whose past social learning experiences have made them highly dependent. Hartup (1958) seems to confirm this when he suggests that, where rejection involves the withholding of positive reinforcers, it appears to intensify dependency.

not love him less but simply had less time to spend with him.

Mat's new experience was one in which his mother shared her love with his sister. His interpretation of this experience, however, was that his mother no longer loved him. The results were frustration, loneliness, depression, and a feeling of abandonment. Unfortunately, his faulty interpretation of his mother's love caused him to use coping strategies which distorted his perception even more. One of the things he learned was that, when he withdrew and became depressed, his mother became concerned. In effect, what he learned was that depression brought attention. Ultimately, however, this type of attention-gaining strategy reinforced the conditions of remorse which were destroying him. As an adult, thirty-six years of age, he repeated these strategies whenever he wanted attention. Since strategies are not only ways of responding to life but include feelings that cue those responses, it was apparent that acting in a depressed way gave him a certain rapport with others which rewarded him for his despondency.

His Destiny. For the most part, Mat seemed intent upon developing a better life, something better for himself and his family. Unfortunately, it was difficult to give up strategies which had been used for so long that they had become an inseparable part of his identity. Thus, he continued to experience those feelings that he had when he was quite young. Although he was intelligent and mature in many respects, there were certain areas within his life that simply never changed (Callis, 1966). Depression was one of those areas. The habit of responding this way also complicated other patterns he had formed over the years and compounded the problem of utilizing his full potential for positive growth.

From working with Mat, it was apparent that he wanted to change. Essentially, he wanted to have experiences which were meaningful. In his own silent way, he searched for a kind of personal identity which would tell others that he, Mat, was here. It was much like a struggle for immortality—not so much to keep on living as to perpetuate the knowledge that he was here. In a sense, his quest was, it seemed, to find his mother's love. When he could find no such love, he attempted suicide. This pattern continued on and on until he finally understood that it was how he perceived the relationship that needed to be changed. Essentially, his major concern was always with what he did not have. Through therapy, he learned to appreciate and enjoy what he did have. The process by which he learned to develop new understandings about those relationships which originally caused the depression was one of reconstruction. It pertained to all of his relationships and particularly to his relationship with his mother.

HIS SEARCH FOR IDENTITY. Watching Mat's psychological growth left the impression that he wanted to change, but he had some reservations about what changes he wanted to make because such changes could be threatening to his total well-being. Indeed, Mat's search seemed like a silent internal struggle for immortality, a desire to have someone acknowledge his presence. It was as if he wanted to cast his shadow deep into the future. Sometimes, it seemed that he was reaching out to touch an eternity of time which had not yet been born. The path of life he traveled was rough and his detours many. Just as his nature was to search and his essence was to experience, so too was it that his identity grew and his relationships matured. Once he learned that all that he was and all that he could be were inseparably tied to his ability to change, he began to risk the challenge of new relationships and to add broader and more meaningful interpretations to old relationships. He accomplished this by testing the fantasies of his relationships against the realities of their existence. It was as he risked himself through reality testing that he eventually found the structural hope upon which he felt he could build a better life.

Watching Mat travel between the fantasy of childhood and the reality of adulthood was a unique study in human strategy. During his childhood, he seemed to search for self-discovery and personal identity. When his baby sister was born, he became confused about his significance and experienced a loneliness that he had never before experienced. As a result, he searched for alternatives, but perhaps because of his age and lack of verbal sophistication, this period of circumspection was more frustrating than his perception of abandonment. He apparently tried desperately to discover new ways to regain his identity with his mother, but at the age of five, the logical search for alternatives was too much for him. Finally, out of desperation, he simply responded in a way which gained his mother's attention.

The way which seemed to work best for both of them was when he withdrew, appeared deeply concerned, was desperately lonely, and grew increasingly remorseful. This response became both a solution and a problem to Mat, primarily because his depression not only brought a quasi sense of love, attention, and identity, but because it taught him that depression was one of the few strategies to which his mother would respond.

When one ponders the reality of this situation, it is not difficult to see that Mat wanted desperately to understand himself and how he related to others. In order to do this, however, he had to find a way to communicate within a world which must have appeared at times to be almost completely impervious to his presence. More important, he had to make decisions about his life and how to reach specific goals. Naturally, the results of such decisions told him something about himself and how successful he was as a decision maker. When he failed to reach the goals he had set for himself, then the way he handled his failures determined what his future would be like.

In Mat's case, he had a close relationship with his mother until his sister was born. He struggled to maintain his relationship with his mother but seemed to get little or no attention from her except when he became depressed. Although he was then rewarded with attention, his choice of strategies was poor because the attention only came with deep depression about his loss of a love object. The only time he received attention was when he was in a state of utter despair. His feelings, unfortunately, turned into a habitual theme. As an adult, his depression existed as the residue of something that occurred many years before. The outcropping of the depression so many years later simply indicated that his strategies were exhausted and that he never really learned how to gain a position of significance without responding as he did when he was a child. The greatest pressure seemed to occur when he was about seventeen. He was just completing high school and was expected to go to work or to college. By now, he had become extremely indecisive about almost everything he did. The pressure created by his constant indecisiveness eventually caused him to seek psychiatric help. Once he did that, the responsibility for failure was not his alone but was shared with his psychiatrist. Thus, depression also became the means by which he could share his responsibilities. He continued to use the services of a psychiatrist for sixteen years. When he finally sought help elsewhere, it was obvious that he wanted to change. Therefore, it is extremely important to note that there was no special magic connected with his remission, but only a desire on his part to be something other than what he was.

HIS MOTHER. The method by which the change was introduced was thematic in nature. Mat first came in for therapy because he claimed that he was impotent, but from the things he said, it seemed more like he married his mother. His wife, Ann, had been carefully molded by his depressive episodes until she responded to him much like he thought he wanted his mother to respond. It seemed apparent that to have such a substitute mother for his wife gave him the opportunity to seek a relationship "closure," the fulfillment he desperately wanted with his mother. Unfortunately, such a substitute never really fulfilled the emptiness generated by the original loss.

Sometimes a person will, through marriage, attempt to gain from his spouse those special attentions he never received from one or both of his parents. It was as Mat ventured into this area during one of his therapy sessions that the significance of his relationship with his mother became obvious. The problem was perhaps compounded by the fact that, as his baby sister grew older, she became a potential substitute for the attention he wanted from his mother. He attempted to construct the same type of loving relationship with his sister that he originally lost with his mother. When she became an adult and married, he felt more abandoned than ever. Imagine, if you can, the sequence of his experiences. First, his mother appeared to have abandoned him for his sister when he was very young. With this feeling of abandonment went the only love, affection, and attention he knew. True, dressing and acting like a boy saved him the embarrassment of being harassed by his playmates but did little to bridge the gap created by the loss of his mother's attention. As a result, the loneliness remained to cause a deep and nagging pain, perhaps even to the extent that Mat never truly appreciated the opportunity he had to assess his own masculinity.

Second, Mat's problem was further compounded by the fact that he tried to reconstruct the positive aspects of his first few years with his mother by using his sister's love as a substitute for his mother's love. Obviously, the substitute never worked because of the sexual overtones.

As his sister grew older, she too seemed to abandon him. The experience was somewhat different because she first dated and later married. Mat's feelings, however, seemed much like those he had when his mother abandoned him. Ultimately, he once again became confused, frustrated, and despondent. Bandura (1960) found that when the mother of a child punished the child's dependency, the child gave up attempting to gain the mother's attention and sought such attention from other people.

Third, his father died when he was in his late teens, thus making his dependency on his mother more critical. It threw a confused youngster into a state of deeper depression. He became extremely unsure of himself and apprehensive about his relations with both men and women. Since he lost the male model he had been following, he gravitated toward a stronger relationship with his uncle. In one of his therapy sessions, he expressed the idea that his uncle ultimately became a symbol of life. It was only when he was with his uncle that he experienced moments of relaxation and enjoyment. For the most part, those moments were rare.

Essentially, what seemed to happen to Mat is that consistent experiences of abandonment made him feel that he could easily be abandoned by others. Thus, in his own innocent way, he began to treat all his relationships as though they were tentative. Even his marriage was dominated by the feelings that his wife would eventually leave. His problem was compounded by the fact that his identity was closely tied to depression, a way of responding to life which discouraged close and meaningful relationships. What he learned from this was that relationships were not safe and that, without any apparent warning, a relationship could be terminated and that he could be abandoned. This knowledge simply increased his depression, for it left him without escape from his web of past experiences. Eventually, he started to take drugs. At first, they seemed to relieve his tension. He no longer had to care about those things in his life which were unresolved. When he finally decided to make a change, his drug habit was the first thing he deserted.

His Road to Depression. During his initial relationship in therapy, Mat talked about his negative feelings toward his wife, his mother, his sister, and others who were in his immediate relationship circle. Because the term "negative" was not clear, the therapist pondered his meaning definitively. As Mat could best explain them, negative feelings were aggressive feelings toward people. He wanted to hurt people without becoming involved in hurting them. That is, he apparently wanted to strike out against certain people but did not want to become an active participant in such an act. Perhaps what he was attempting to say was that he wanted to destroy the same people through whom he sought his personal identity, but because he needed them, he could not destroy them. Yet, the desire to destroy them was almost as strong as the need to identify through them. Depressives frequently live through others. Unfortunately, this deprives them of the opportunity to gain their own identity. Thus, as depressives, they become entrapped. They typically use people as a means of self-identity. Yet, they realize as they do so that to seek identity through someone else is to deny themselves the pleasure of their own identity. At this point in Mat's therapy, an algorithmic schematic of his learning route looked like this (*see* Fig. 5):

His Life-Style. These experiences with Mat seem to reflect three basic phases of his development which are extremely important. First, his philosophy of life gave direction to his thinking and what he hoped for in the future. Second, his perception of life left some impression of how he felt about the experiences he had. Third, his life-style gave some indication of how he planned to reach his goals and to what extent his previous experiences molded the path by which he would travel.

MAT'S PRIMARY LEARNING ROUTE

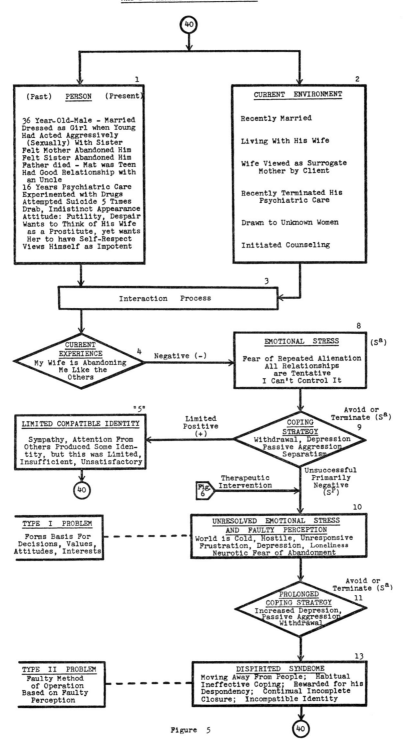

Figure 5

In practice, his philosophy of life had to serve as the basis for his decisions. By understanding his philosophy, it was possible to study the method by which he coped with difficulties, failure, inadequacies, and delays. His coping strategies served as the basic ingredient for the mask he was wearing. Each time he embarked on a journey designed to take him deeper into life, the direction he took, the attitude he held, and the determination he maintained served as the basis for his next decision.

Equally important is the fact that Mat's philosophy of life served as the basis for the way he related with others—how he accepted others, shared with others, and loved others. The principles which governed his philosophy were, for the most part, ethics. They told him what was "right" or "wrong," "good" or "bad," and "proper" or "improper." As he began to understand these constructs, he also developed a sense of morals or a baseline concept of life which told him to what extent he practiced those constructs. Since his morality was a personal reaction to such constructs, it gave him some idea of how close to or far away from these constructs he was. To this extent, Mat's value system was shaped both by the way he lived his life and by his desire to subscribe to or deviate from those constructs or standards which governed his society. Whenever these two aspects of his life were incongruent, he experienced tension. Thus, one must assume that Mat's constructs were based on what he perceived yet were incompatible with the reality of what existed. This incompatibility resulted in tension. Since he could neither resolve nor ignore those factors which led to his tension, he found himself in trouble. The way he handled it was by assuming strategies which typically define depression. This does not mean that he did not experience real depression, but rather, that he learned that, with his feelings of depression, he sometimes received attention. Unfortunately, once he gained attention in this way, his depression usually destroyed the relationship. Yet, for Mat, there was always some question about whether or not any relationship was possible without depression.

RISK: THE KEY TO CHANGE

Mat's struggle for change was much like a game of chance. The name of the game was life. In order to win, he had to risk. What he learned to risk was himself. It was as he contemplated risking himself and gaining new and different experiences that he realized that through risk he could also fail. This frightened him at first. He knew that he wanted to change, but was not sure of what he would lose as he made the effort. He also recognized that without trying, he could never succeed. His struggle was painful. Mat questioned whether or not to leave conditions of the past or to attempt to reconstruct his life. He became terribly apprehensive about change because it involved new experiences and new attitudes toward old experiences. Eventually, however, he came to the conclusion that it was better to make an effort and fail than never to have tried. He came to this conclusion after exploring his life and discovering that attempting new values, interests, and attitudes was better than having values, interests, and attitudes which simply did not work. He concluded that, by risking, he did indeed win because he became a participant in life rather than a spectator. No matter how many failures he had, his new outlook on life made him aware of the fact that each new experience could bring him closer to his purpose for living.

To Mat, this meant that the consequences of the experience became less important than having the experience. If things did not turn out as he had hoped, he would simply attempt to convert his failures into success, recognizing that each experience brought him closer to a completeness within his own life.

He felt that the key to understanding life was in terms of how he treated the consequences of his experiences. If he made the most of an experience, it made him feel good. Each experience became a challenge, and with each challenge, he attempted to make his life more complete. This in turn helped him to find identity and gave him the feeling that he could establish realistic goals toward which he could work.

What appears to happen as a person searches for identity is that he has multiple experiences, each of which leaves an imprint. For Mat, those experiences caused feelings with which he could not deal. Although he was not always completely aware of each experience, the impact of each experience was recorded within his self-system. These experiences then produced the values to which he subscribed. His problem was to organize and maintain the unity of his system. Once an experience became part of the system, it became an inseparable part of Mat's life. The strategies he used were those which appeared to help him to stabilize while struggling with actions which were incompatible with his feelings. It appears that those experiences which were meaningful to him were quickly assimilated into his system, while those which were incompatible or less meaningful became the stimuli for future change. The nucleus around which the system functioned was based on the experiences he had and the values he held.

THE PRESS TECHNIQUE. How Mat grew from these experiences and attempted to move forward in life dictated, to a great extent, how he felt about himself and others. Once he understood that his interpretations of certain experiences in life were inaccurate, his attitude toward those experiences changed. He was able to make such changes because he was willing to examine the sharp similarities or differences between what he was saying and the reality of what happened. This is a technique which psychoanalysts refer to as *juxtaposition*. In nexus psychotherapy, it is referred to as a press technique through which the therapist draws sharp contrasts between two statements by juxtaposing the two statements so that they can be examined by comparison. The idea is based on the humanistic belief that the constructive forces which lead to change reside primarily within man and that anything he values must first become an integrated part of his total system. As a result of his perceptual inaccuracies, Mat made mistakes. That is, he realized that what he perceived and the reality of what truly existed were sometimes diametrically opposed. This made his reaction to experiences faulty. As he began to understand this, he said,

> I've been thinking about my sister and her criticism of me.
> (pause) My first impression was that she meant that I was no
> good. At first, I felt anger — then despair (pause). I thought
> about her relationship with my mother. When my mother gave
> her so much attention, I felt terribly defeated — but I guess I

was terribly defeated to start with. The impression I got — that is the interpretation I had of it — was that my sister was saying that I — ah — couldn't compete.

"What does that mean?" asked the therapist.

Well, what it meant to me was that I couldn't win. This was my interpretation — you know, it wasn't real but only what I thought. (pause) Since then, I've learned that she wasn't competing at all.

"I'm not sure what that means, Mat," said the therapist.

What it means is that we talked about it just the other night and I realized for the first time how wrong I was. Both about my sister and my mother.

"Oh!" said the thearpist.

Yeah I guess what I want you to know is that I know how wrong I was. (pause) I guess all that anger was wasted. But you know what I've been doing is to claim defeat before I've earned it.

"So what is it you're trying to tell me, Mat?" asked the therapist.

"It seems that what you're saying is that no one can defeat you because you've already defeated yourself. (pause) I wonder what purpose it serves for you to handle competition in this way?"

Ah, I don't really know. I guess what I'm saying is that, if I accept defeat before I get started, then I don't have to compete. Lately, since I've talked to you, I've been trying to find out how real some of my thoughts are. I ask people, you know. Instead of like I did before — just thinking something about someone. But ah — sometimes it's painful. (pause) I sometimes think that, if I give up, it won't be so painful. (pause) Well, that's not true — I know now what I have to do. That is, I know it's painful, but I know that, when I do it, there's a way out — there's a tomorrow. You know, when I felt "down," I just tried to fight it — kind of inside. It seemed like life was hopeless — like something was telling me life was hopeless.

"Something?" asked the therapist.

Yeah, me, I guess.

"I wonder why you'd do that?" asked the therapist.

Well, I guess sometimes I want sympathy.

"Oh," said the therapist, "and do you get it?"

(pause)   Well, ah — no.   Sometimes I feel that it works, but then later, I find out that it really doesn't.   Like with my mother, I tried to get her to be sympathetic — but it didn't work.   I guess now that I think about it, it's not even what I wanted.   (pause) But anyway, when I didn't get it (sympathy), life seemed hopeless.   That's what I mean when I say despair and — hopeless — that I was hopelessly trying to get my mother to give me more attention.   But she didn't.   Mostly because she couldn't. (pause)   She didn't even know — that is, she thought we had a good thing going.   Anyway, it was easier to sulk than to act angry.

"And probably more acceptable, too," said the therapist.

Yeah, I'm sure.   I suppose that's what I'm talking about when I talk about my sister and my brother-in-law.   I've used feelings of despair to get sympathy from my mother and my sister.   It seems when I feel this way that I do it for attention.   I think that my actions are prompted by my faulty interpretations of how they feel.   Since they don't really feel like that (like Mat thought they did), they don't pay much attention to my despair — 'cause there's no reason to have it.   Does that make sense?

"Does it to you?" asked the therapist.

Well, I learned a way of life — I told myself I'm no good, I'm going to fail.   I did those things to get attention and to take pressure off.   At least, that's what I think I've been doing.

Then, after I started to look at what I was doing, I learned something else.   (pause)   I learned that people aren't feeling — or, ah thinking what I thought.   (pause)   Knowing this made me feel better about myself.

To a certain extent, I'm still like I was — even now — to a degree, I still feel life is hopeless.

"I'm not sure what that means," said the therapist.

Well, I think I'm using that figure of speech right now to get your sympathy.   (pause)   In a way I think you already know that, and to that extent, what I'm doing is self-defeating.   It serves no purpose — (pause) and still, it must.

"Perhaps," said the therapist, "what you're doing is learning to relate with people at a level commensurate with your age."

Yeah, I can see that.   What you're telling me is that I've grown physically but that, in some ways, I still relate to my sister and mother like I did when I was five or six years old. (pause) I can see that I'm mature in some ways but like a child in others. Yeah, I can see that and when I relate to adults, I ah — do the same things I did when I was young. It was something that didn't work when I was young and doesn't work now. But it's all I have. (pause) It was all I had. (pause) That's what I'm learning, isn't it? I'm learning to do something I should have learned to do a long time ago. I'm — ah — it's not really a question of failure — it's a matter of growing up — how to find success.

ANALYZING MAT'S STATEMENTS.   It is interesting to note that Mat's thinking covers two basic patterns.   The first deals with Mat's inner feelings of abandonment, loss, and hopelessness in his relationship with his mother.

His second pattern deals with his overt relationship with his mother, sister, and brother-in-law. Knowing this, it was, obvious that his attitude toward relationships had to be changed.   In his efforts to change, he tested what he perceived about people against the reality of what they were truly communicating.   The method by which change was encouraged was the press technique.   As a result of pressing Mat and challenging his previous values, his attitudes toward people changed, and with that change, he incorporated a new approach to relating.   He found as he changed his behavior that when he related positively to people, they responded positively to him.   A general representation of some significant areas of Mat's attitudinal orientation, which appeared receptive to change via nexus psychotherapy, can be seen in Figure 6.

A third pattern that reversed itself had to do with work.   The one thing that Mat always dreaded was applying for a job.   At the time he came for therapy, he was a trained technician.   Because he never felt competent in his field, however, he shifted jobs regularly.   During recent years, he had not worked at all.   Shortly after his first few therapy sessions, he applied for a job.   He received the job and continued to hold it throughout his therapy.   The drop-out theme was reversed primarily by taking him through each experience of work, challenging the fantasies of his thinking, and encouraging the realities of experiencing.   Each time a potential for failure seemed possible, it was explored in terms of what could be done

Segment Of

TYPE I PROBLEM INTERVENTION

With "Mat"

24

```
ATTITUDES AND PERCEPTIONS RECEPTIVE TO CHANGE
```

1. Inner Feelings of Abandonment, Loss, and Hopelessness in His Relationship With His Mother.
2. Feelings Regarding His Sister and Her Husband.
3. Fear of Failure and Depression Due to Anticipated Failure and Rejection.
4. Self-Doubt and Attitudes Toward Work.
5. Feelings of Sexual Impotence and Inadequacy.
6. Feelings of Futility and Despair Regarding the Future.
7. Luck or Fate is in Control and Determines Outcome, as Opposed to Personal Action and Responsibility for Consequences.
8. Avoidance of New Experiences and Concomitant Personal Withdrawal.
9. Relationship of Withdrawal, Sulking, and Depressive State to Eliciting Sympathy, Attention, and other Such "Proofs of Love."
10. Depression Resulting From His Desire to Be Close to People Complicated by His Fear of Abandonment Once He Becomes Emotionally Attached to Someone.

PRESS   25
"Perceptual Chipping"

26

```
JUXTAPOSITION
```

1. You Were Defeated to Start With Because Your Mother Gave More Attention to Your Sister.
2. Yet, You Seem to Say No One Can Defeat You Because You've Already Defeated Yourself.
1. I Want Sympathy. . .It Was Easier to Sulk Than to Act Angry.
2. And Probably More Acceptable Too!
1. I Still Feel Life Is Hopeless. . . I Say That to Get Your Sympathy.
2. Perhaps You're Learning to Relate at a Level Commensurate Your Age.

27

```
RECAPITULATION
```

1. You Now Seem to be Responding to Your Wife Just as You Previously Said You Responded to Your Mother.

2. You Appear to Keep Going Back to the Time When You Were About Five Years Old to Reiterate Your Feelings of Abandonment, Thus You Must Relate This to What You Now Feel.

28

```
CONSEQUENCES
```

Maybe I've Prevented Positive Growth by Clinging to an Immature Sense of Security. The Future is Potentially Better, But to Achieve it Requires Change and Change Requires Risking. My Sulking to Get Love and Attention Brought Some Reinforcement, But it is Immature and Self-Defeating. My Negative Approach Produced a Cycle of Self-Fulfilling Prophecy.

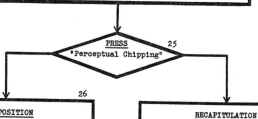

Figure 6

in the event that such failure did occur. When necessary, role playing and role reversal were used to reality test within the safety of the therapeutic relationship those wants that did or might take place while working.

MAT AS A PERSON OF HABIT. Philosophically speaking, it seems safe to say that Mat was a person of habit. In Mat's case, experience became the nucleus around which his total life moved. In a sense, his value system was the center of his existence and changed only as he reached out to surrender himself to new adventures. He once said, "I'm learning to trust myself, but I find it difficult. There are times when I'm not convinced I won't fail. Yet, when I think about it, I know that my first failure will always come from not trying."

Failure was, for Mat, a way of life. It permitted him to withdraw, to hide, and to seek seclusion whenever anything challenging came into his life. To that extent, it became his pattern; it was constant enough to indicate what direction he was taking in life and what difficulties could be anticipated. Understanding this pattern made it possible to know where Mat was going simply by knowing where he had been.

METALANGUAGE: A KEY TO UNDERSTANDING

Actually, relating has always seemed much like an art of growing together. It requires sensitivity, compassion, understanding, love, acceptance, integrity, and positive regard. Yet, these ingredients are difficult to define. The difficulty stems from the fact that part of every definition rests within the perceiver. Berne (1972) once referred to what we describe as metalanguage as a covert transaction which occurs when people say one thing and mean another.

Love, for example, might be recognized as a feeling of passion. Yet, how a person uses the term has much to do with how he feels about himself and how secure he feels. Thus, the art of relating is less easily defined than is the science of relating. This must seem terribly confusing to a neophyte therapist, primarily because he wants to understand as much as he can about how to relate. The key to understanding relationships as an art is basically one of listening. It is not so much what the person is saying as what he is alluding to—his metalanguage. For example, several years ago, Arnold Lazarus did a tape which he used to illustrate his technique in behavior therapy. Essentially, the tape deals with a man who is extremely jealous of his wife. Although Lazarus was seemingly treating the patient's jealousy by extinguishing his fears about how his wife related to other men, there is a metalanguage here which leaves the impression that his newly found tolerance toward her possible infidelities might really be an expression of his depersonalization in the relationship. It also poses the interesting thought "What if his jealousy was really a reflection of his inability to perform well sexually?"

In Mat's case, to decipher his metalanguage was, as Tyler (1972) so aptly put it, to understand the message behind the words. When Mat said, "Sometimes I feel that it works, but then later, I find out it really doesn't," it seemed that he was saying, "I continue to do things that don't work—I wonder why?" The thought going through the therapist's mind at that point was that he was obviously torn between doing things as he had in the past because it seemed safe but realizing that he must change because, in reality, it wasn't safe at all. To the therapist, this meant that, although Mat wanted to change, there were also reasons for wanting to remain the same. He was confronted with two alternatives; one promised a potentially better future but demanded a change. The other promised him a false sense of security which offered no future.

When he said, "I use to try to get her to be sympathetic—but it didn't work," it seemed like he had exhausted all alternatives. His follow-up statements, however, indicated that, although that period of his life seemed hopeless, he had since found other alternatives. To this extent, therapy appeared to be of some value to him, and as a result, his therapist took this to mean that he was once again hopeful and searching for a more complete life. This is one of the key concepts in nexus therapy, *i.e.* helping a client to reach a point where he is ready and willing to utilize his total potential to go beyond where he is.

Because Mat was deeply depressed when he first asked for

therapy, it seemed obvious that his gradual change from an attitude of helplessness to one of hopefulness indicated that he was once again ready to assert himself. He was ready to risk himself. His attitude toward life changed because he felt that he could accomplish more by having new experiences than he could by repeating old habits. That desire for change combined with some understandings about who he was and how such change could be brought about made it possible for him to risk finding greater personal identity.

One of the responsibilities of his therapist was to create a climate which was conducive to growth. A second responsibility was to help him to understand how to achieve maximum effectiveness when the results of his decisions were not what he expected.

Essentially, Mat had to learn several things throughout his therapeutic relationship. First, he had to recognize the fact that he had a talent for many things in life he had never tried. Second, he had to learn to experience as many new things as possible realizing that, by so doing, he was expanding his own world and, therefore, his ability to find his own personal identity within that world. Third, he had to recognize that decisions about new experiences in his life were risky, but that, without such risk, he could neither change nor grow. Fourth, Mat had to realize that each new experience, in order to be completely fulfilling, would have to bring satisfaction to himself and benefit to society. Without such balance, complete fulfillment would not be possible. Fifth, he had to learn to deal with failure. That is, he had to recognize that any risk could lead to failure. Therefore, it was imperative for him to understand persistence and to recognize that success comes when and if one persists.

In order to help Mat achieve these objectives, it was necessary that there be some scientific basis from which to work. The development of such a basis is what might be referred to as the Science of Understanding. This involves an objective approach to understanding a person and a systematic approach for bringing about change. It also provides a method by which the theoretical concepts in Chapters 1, 2, and 3 can be related to the practical aspects of therapy.

CHAPTER 5

NEXUS PSYCHOTHERAPY AS A SCIENCE OF UNDERSTANDING

THEORETICALLY, ALL HUMANS develop a system by which they function. Because the system is relatively constant, understanding the system helps to understand the person.

DEPRESSION AS A COPING STRATEGY

In Mat's case, there seemed to be a good deal of depression. That meant that he could be expected to function in certain specific ways. Quite generally, his dialogue indicated that his depression was characterized by a definite loss of interest in setting goals and in living. He complained of an inability to concentrate on those things that seemed an essential part of moving ahead in life. Many of his thoughts were dedicated to his past, how poorly his life had gone, and how futile it had been. He resented and withdrew from the challenges of decision making and responsibility taking. Because the results of his decisions seldom worked out as he planned, he felt that life was rather hopeless. At least some of his time was spent thinking about death and whether or not it might be a way out. Much of the time, he felt that no one cared about him, and frequently he felt that he could never make any real contribution to anyone or anything. At times, his inability to cope led to physical reactions such as a loss of appetite, marked nervousness, and excessive fatigue, all of which telegraphed the idea that the climate in which he lived was not conducive to healthy growth (Mendels, 1970).

In a sense, what Mat was saying was that, since life had not gone well, it was best to withdraw. One way of doing that was to avoid making decisions. That meant that he had to get others to

84

make decisions for him. To the extent that he could accomplish this end, he continued to withdraw.

In his relationship with the therapist, his emphasis shifted from withdrawal to assertiveness. The method by which this was accomplished was by helping him to understand that much of what he did was related to how well he understood his experiences and how good his method of responding was, once such experiences occurred. Observation indicated that, for Mat, just as is true for most people, the number of alternatives that he could pursue was rather limited (Callis, 1966). In an effort to survive, he used those coping strategies which he thought would help him. Depression and all those characteristics which described his depressive mood were the coping strategies which he used to sustain himself. Unfortunately, they worked, but only as sustainers of emotional stress not as enhancers of emotional stability. As a result, he had to change, but before change became possible, he had to recognize how he had misinterpreted many of his experiences and how, as a result of that misinterpretation, he had developed a faulty process of responding. The technique used to turn a person around in nexus therapy is referred to as a press technique.

THE PRESS TECHNIQUE

Essentially, perceptual chipping is the basis for the press technique. That is, it permits a counselor or therapist the opportunity to keep his client relegated to self-examination. It is the basis by which a client is forced to look at himself and to explore his potential for change. For example, when Mat said, ". . . it was easier to sulk than to act angry," the therapist responded with "and probably more acceptable, too." This was a press. What Mat was forced to do was to look at his coping strategy and how it worked. His mother did not tolerate angry outbursts, and therefore, he learned to resort to a strategy which was acceptable to both of them. He may even have learned this by mistake. That is, from what Mat said later, it appeared that he was punished for acting out against his mother. In his frustration, he learned to sulk. Obviously, sulking was simply not knowing how to respond. When his mother saw his despair, she apparently showed concern.

This concern served as a reward, and Mat continued to feel despair each time he wanted attention.

Analyzing the case of Mat in this way, it appears that there are three major ideas which serve to stimulate a theoretical persuasion in psychotherapy.

(1) First, it seems that at least one approach to theory can be built on the concept of how to develop total utilization of the multidimensional potential man has for growth. This means that long-range personality change can be self-initiated through attitudinal change once the person becomes flexible enough in his thinking to recognize alternative courses of action and how they can serve in his best interests.

In Mat's case, alternatives were not easily discernible until he changed his attitude toward his early life experiences. His change obviously prompted a change in those with whom he related. The positive responses by others toward his change served to reinforce his belief that the change was good. The change was further reinforced by reducing the tension that had existed when his relationships with others were strained.

(2) Second, it seems that therapy must become more refined as a science if it is to be taught with any hope for outcome consistency (Eysenck, 1966). This is not to say that it must be a dogma, but rather that it must define for practitioners the phenomena or events of concern which are theoretically meaningful. Further, it must define the consistency with which such events occur, and finally, it must deal with objectives toward which responses to such events ultimately lead.

In Mat's case, he used specific coping strategies to survive. He felt that what he was doing was in his best interests, but requested psychotherapy when he could no longer cope by himself. His pattern of coping gave a general impression of his direction in life and what he hoped to accomplish during specific phases of his life. This in turn gave some indication of what his values were like and where his deficiencies were. Perceptual chipping challenged him to reexamine his attitudes and to explore the reality with which they could be applied to his total life process. Once he accepted this challenge, he found that reality testing could help him to understand how well he could accept the consequences. If he found the consequences acceptable, he then accepted the change as part of his total system of functioning.

(3) Third, it seems that psychotherapy must employ those concepts which are rational and consistent. This means that, regardless of what school of thought a therapist subscribes to, his theory must work, and it must work with consistency —not only for him, but for other counselors and psychotherapists who follow the theory.

What this really means is that there must be a system or classification scheme into which events of concern can be ordered. It appears that a system is "good" when it follows a method which can be learned and applied. However, it also appears that such a system runs the risk of (a) forcing people into molds and/or (b) subscribing to a constellation of understandings or ideas which are basically faulty.

Yet, to disregard a systematic approach to therapy would give the therapist no point of departure from which to work. When this occurs, the therapist fails to understand where the relationship is and where it is going.

In the case of Mat, his patterns of conversation gave a general indication of where he was, and his coping strategies gave some indication of how he was attempting to deal with life. Once this was understood, perceptual chipping helped him to understand his potential for change. To become something other than what he was, he kept reality testing his new attitudes in an effort to discover how comfortable he could be with such change.

IMPLEMENTING BEHAVIOR CHANGE

Theory is, by definition, a manifestation of the basic postulates from which man works to "confirm or refute" certain specific hypotheses. In this particular instance, it can be assumed that Mat was a growing, changing entity and that, as such, he had a specific nature. For all practical purposes, it can further be assumed that he was much like other people. It was obvious that he wanted a better life but would have trouble reaching that objective unless he could integrate his experiences into his total system of functioning. It was obvious that he exercised limited control over his behavior because he was not totally aware of his full potential for change. His ability to explore alternatives leading to change depended on his flexibility, *i.e.* his ability to (a) form new attitudes when necessary, (b) form new objectives when necessary, or (c) form new attitudes and new objectives if it appeared necessary for ultimate growth.

To this extent, Mat was the captain of his fate; he could make choices about how he wanted to move and in what directions he wanted to go but could not select courses of action which had not yet entered his repertoire of thought. He was, therefore, restricted by self-limiting experiences. This did not restrict his responsibility for decisions made but did, to a degree, restrict his success when he made decisions. To this end, he was responsible for his decisions but not limited to alternatives except by his own inflexibility. His life was, therefore, shaped not only through his experiences but in terms of how he responded to those experiences and how his environment then influenced those response patterns.

To this extent, his nature appeared to be experiential. As a child, he searched to find out how each object and experience could become a meaningful part of his life. To this end, much of what he did was born out of a need for closure, the discovery of how he related to each thing he experienced. Ultimately, however, he was influenced by the impact of his experiences on his total existence, *i.e.* how his responses to these experiences made him appear to others, and how these experiences in and by themselves made him feel personally.

The nucleus of the system through which these experiences were transmitted and processed was his mind. Essentially, his mind influenced what he was, for it coordinated the existence of his present physical being with his total spiritual being.

The residue of the system through which these experiences became manifest in action was a reflection of what Mat thought, felt, and feared. This was his personality. It was the way he responded to life and how he used the resulting experiences in the best interests of the goals he hoped to achieve.

The process by which he learned to respond was the process by which he filtered out those things he felt were least essential to his total system of functioning and by which he integrated those things he felt were most necessary to his well being. Learning, in its most basic form, was the process by which Mat judged the experiences he was having. Values were the residue of that process. To this extent, they were the essence of the process by which his attitudes were changed or maintained. Mat's values were, in a sense, his *raison d'être*. In practice, he repeated those things which he felt had helped him and avoided those things he felt had not. His justification for his actions became his philosophy of life. When he lacked a sense of harmony between his inner feelings about himself and the way he responded toward others, he was in trouble. Such incongruencies created within him feelings of despair. It was this conflicting struggle between what he felt and what he did which caused emotional stress and eventuated in chaotic patterns of decision making.

THE THERAPIST'S ROLE

Both the experiences Mat had and the way he responded were important to therapy. Knowledge of such patterns made it possible to understand how Mat was perceiving his experiences. Therapy made it possible to explore his intentions. Through the use of a press technique, it was then possible to chip away at those attitudes which seemed to be faulty or prevented greater flexibility in Mat's thinking. Apparently, his faulty perception had much to do with his method of responding. When he was unsuccessful, it was assumed that this method of responding was faulty because his understanding of the experience had been misinterpreted.

BEYOND THE MASK. People like Mat sometimes compromise themselves by subscribing to acts which are incompatible with their feelings. When they do this, they apparently mask their real feelings hoping that, by so doing, others will accept them. Mat had to become aware of this and then understand why the incompatibility existed and what to do about it. It might be said that Mat never learned an acceptable way of relating. What he thought pleased others did not please him, primarily because it caused him to mask his true feelings. The internal struggle between what he felt and the way he reacted caused him considerable frustration. His pattern of responding through his depressive moods gave a vivid impression of how well his coping strategies were working. What Mat imagined much of the time was that he was performing before a highly critical audience of peers. Apparently, he felt that he could not abide by the rules of these peers. This was simply because the rules were not clear. As a result, he assumed a role he felt that his societal peers wanted him to assume. When he did this, he sacrificed a portion of his own identity in order to be accepted by society. Unfortunately, he never received that acceptance. His world became one of confusion primarily because he could not resolve the conflict between what he wanted for himself and what he thought society wanted from him.

To resolve this conflict through therapy he explored each situation or conflict realistically in terms of (a) what he did, (b) what he felt he should have done, and (c) what alternatives he felt he had. The focus of his exploration was on how correctly he perceived situations which led to conflict. This provided additional flexibility in his thinking by helping him to recognize those experiences which were not accurately perceived. Changed perception then led to new alternatives for dealing with his wife, mother, sister, and other relatives.

The basis for his feelings emerged from his value system which, in turn, seemed to be a reflection of his philosophy of life. Once Mat felt differently toward people, he noticed that they responded differently toward him. Essentially, what he accomplished during therapy was the ability to enter into close personal relations with others without the threat of disconfirmation if the relationships were terminated. The philosophical basis for this new attitude seemed to be capsuled by a statement he made during one of his sessions:

> Unless I can be myself in a relationship, no one knows who I am. They (people) react to my mask. (pause) That makes it

difficult for me to know who I am. (pause) For some reason, I thought it was better to mask. Now I know that I have to risk being what I am.

If people don't like what I am when I risk, I can still work on liking them. What's important is for me to do that — to learn to like them for the best that's in them. I guess if a guy doesn't like me, he has to deal with his own "hang-ups" just like I do.

Statements like this indicate that Mat was moving toward a relationship with himself which was more comfortable for him. These and other more adaptive attitudinal shifts are graphically depicted in Figure 7. In his earlier sessions, he was less capable of dealing with his future and continued to gravitate toward the past. He was overly concerned about failure and extremely cautious about new experiences. His attitude was self-encapsulating. It kept him from having experiences which could have made his life more meaningful. By his interpretation, however, what his attitude did best of all was to protect him from failure. Basically, the realities from which failure emerged were nothing more than fantasies Mat had about his life and the people in it. By contrast, in his initial relationship with the therapist, Mat said:

I'm so afraid of failure that I don't even try a second time.[1] (pause) You know what I mean? I don't try because I'm afraid to fail.[2] (pause) I don't believe in the old proverb — "Try, try again" — once I fail, that's it.[3] (pause) Even though I may try again, I think, "Well, why try? You'll just fail."[4] I don't have any self-confidence.[5] I have to be tricked into doing things.[6] Then, when something goes right, I say, "Did I really do that or was it just luck?"[7] I can't even develop self-confidence.[8]

Numbering these statements makes it possible to convey how an in-depth analysis of Mat's statements works. Based on the theory from which nexus therapy emerges, the following analysis seems appropriate:

(a) Mat's first three statements reflect a fear of failure.
(b) The fourth reflects a sense of depression over anticipated failure.
(c) The fifth reflects self-doubt and feelings of inadequacy.

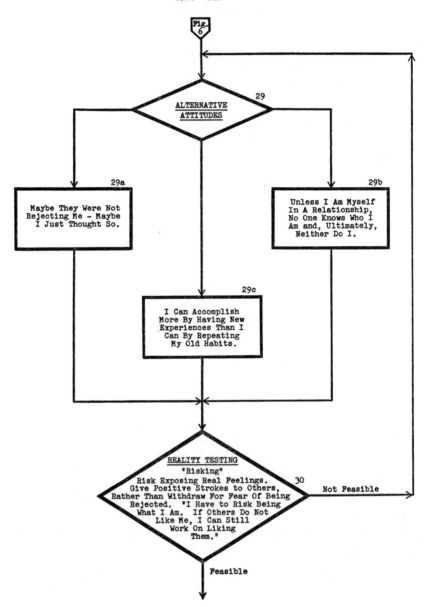

Segment Of

TYPE I PROBLEM INTERVENTION

With "Mat"

Fig. 6

ALTERNATIVE ATTITUDES — 29

29a
Maybe They Were Not Rejecting Me - Maybe I Just Thought So.

29b
Unless I Am Myself In A Relationship, No One Knows Who I Am and, Ultimately, Neither Do I.

29c
I Can Accomplish More By Having New Experiences Than I Can By Repeating My Old Habits.

REALITY TESTING
"Risking"
Risk Exposing Real Feelings. Give Positive Strokes to Others, Rather Than Withdraw For Fear Of Being Rejected. "I Have to Risk Being What I Am. If Others Do Not Like Me, I Can Still Work On Liking Them." — 30

Not Feasible

Feasible

Figure 7

(d) The sixth reflects a sense of futility.

(e) The seventh and eighth reflect self-doubt and futility.

Note how negative those statements are. The more emotional stress a person feels, the more negative his comments. A careful evaluation of other statements by Mat indicates two things: First, he is struggling desperately for survival and his struggle appears to be between his objectives and the process by which he attempts to reach those objectives. That is, his desire for his mother's love and the method by which he attempts to get that love.   Second, Mat apparently could not explore alternative courses of action at the inception of his relationship with his therapist because he did not possess the sophistication to examine his life process objectively. Therefore, what he did was to repeat his mistakes rather than to change his method of responding or his objectives. His constant struggle without success probably reinforced his feelings of failure.

This understanding is extremely important because it illustrates, to some degree, the idea that what people say and do is closely related to what they are and how they are attempting to deal with themselves and others. Obviously, perception becomes the nucleus of man's thinking, for it is both the seat of experiential ingestion and the "synapse" of personal reaction. Thus, when Mat's method of functioning was faulty, it was because his perceptual understandings were faulty. Getting Mat to understand this required self-examination on his part and the willingness to change on the basis of what he found. The therapeutic process by which such change is implemented is confrontation, the art of getting a person to recognize his own mistakes and then correct them. It requires working out a new life-style based on new understandings. This is done in conjunction with a counselor or therapist. The therapist's primary responsibility is to get the person with whom he is working to examine and reexamine his life-style and to discern from this examination where he may have made mistakes of faulty interpretations. Once the person understands this, he can test this understanding against reality. His method for reality testing may, at first, be examined in his relationship with the therapist and later generalized to other significant people in his life.

During Mat's initial therapy session, several things became obvious. Apparently, he was saying that he wanted to try again but only if the conditions were right. By contrast, he was also saying he did not want to try at all. That is, at one point, he said. "I'm so afraid of failure that I *don't* even try a second time. (pause) I *don't* try because I'm afraid to fail." Later he said, "Even though I may try again, I think, "Well, why try? You'll just fail.""

Although these are negative inferences, they hold much hope for any therapist because Mat is not saying *won't* but *don't*. This, combined with his statement, "Even though I may try again," is a form of metalanguage which seems to be saying, "If you can show me how to reach my objectives without experiencing pain or fear or if you can help me to learn how to participate in new experiences without feeling threatened, then I'll try again."

Obviously, Mat fears making decisions because he anticipates failure. He also realizes that without making decisions he cannot move ahead in life and, therefore, cannot reach his objectives.

When he said, "Once I fail, that's it." The futility of his statement leads one to believe that life is absolutely hopeless. Yet, failure is a part of every life and may even be a significant part of success. Thus, it becomes obvious that Mat has to learn how to utilize his failure in the best interests of success. He has to learn to profit from his mistakes.

Then, too, his statement, "I have to be tricked into doing things," seems to be a "cushion" for failure. What he really seems to be saying here is that, if he makes a decision and fails, it should not be his fault because he was tricked. That provides him with an emotional "cushion"; it gives him something on which he can place the blame for failure. This was, in fact, part of his statement dealing with luck and seemed to convey the message that "being tricked" or having "luck" is responsible for everything and Mat for nothing. Yet, by virtue of the depression he experienced, it appears that to trust one's life to the unpredictable realm of fate could, by itself, be a very disconcerting experience. Thus, it also seemed that Mat was, in a sense, saying that he wanted to become his own person. How he patterned his thinking and how this pattern reflected the success or failure of his coping strategies seemed essential to psychotherapy. Therefore, it was necessary to understand what he was saying, what he felt, and what his intentions were.

Although most of these eight statements indicated depression, his statement, "Even though I may try again," served as a declaration which held out hope. What Mat seemed to be saying was that, if he could find a way of life free of failure or one that helped him to deal with failure effectively, he would be willing to try again.

The therapist's initial statement was, "What is failure, Mat?" He paused, sat there for several minutes thinking about it, and finally said:

I don't really know. I guess it's the way I feel about something.

"Something," repeated his therapist.

Yeah, life I suppose — maybe the way I feel about how I've handled my life. (pause) I don't feel good about it.

This initial statement deals with a definitive approach to understanding. It required that Mat define for his therapist as well as for himself the specific criteria by which he condemned himself as a failure. The purpose it served was to help Mat organize his thoughts and to recognize that, without his values, the concept "failure" was only a word. Until it was defined in terms of his pragmatic experiences, it had no meaning at all. Knowing that he felt he had not handled life well opened up a new area for exploration. Therefore, the therapist responded to his last remark by saying,

"And how have you handled your life, Mat?"

Poorly, I think. I haven't accomplished anything.

"What is it you're suppose to accomplish?" asked the therapist.

I wish I knew. Maybe that's why I'm here.

Realizing that Mat had to explore more deeply, the therapist said, "I'm not sure I understand what you're saying, Mat. Maybe you're so concerned with what you haven't accomplished that it is difficult to appreciate what you have accomplished."

Yeah, that's true, but I feel down all the time.

"Tell me about that feeling," said the therapist.

I feel lonely.   (pause)   I feel despair.   I'm not sure about how others feel about me.

"Others," said the therapist.

Yeah, especially my mother and my sister.

From this point on, he talked about his relationships with his mother, sister, brother-in-law, and wife.   These topics became major areas of concentration, during which, the person with whom he attempted to deal most frequently was his mother. Therefore, it was assumed that his mother was a key figure in his depression.   Pursuing an understanding of his relationship with his mother soon led Mat to realize that many of the things he did as an adult were generalizations developed out of his childhood.   The real problem was that they were based on his perception of the experiences he had and the personal interpretations he attached to these experiences as a child.   Although his feelings were genuine, the understandings upon which they were based were, in many cases, simply not true.

What sometimes seems to happen is that people base part of their understandings on such things as speculation, fantasy, or anticipation.   This means that, no matter what a person experiences, part of his interpretation about that experience may be faulty.   With Mat, it became obvious that he felt that his mother had abandoned him.   Going back to his mother and discussing his feelings made him realize that he had misjudged his mother. Understanding that he had misinterpreted this relationship as a child, he realized that he may well have made similar mistakes about other relationships.   Then, too, he realized that, because he was still relating to others much like he did when he was a child, he could still be making similar mistakes as an adult.   Recognizing this helped him to change his attitude toward people.   The change was reinforced by the positive responses it brought from others and he was soon on his way to a more stable life.   A portion of Mat's therapeutic movement prefacing the critical nexus intervention into his faulty coping strategies is presented in Figure 8.

Segment Of

TYPE II PROBLEM INTERVENTION

With "Mat"

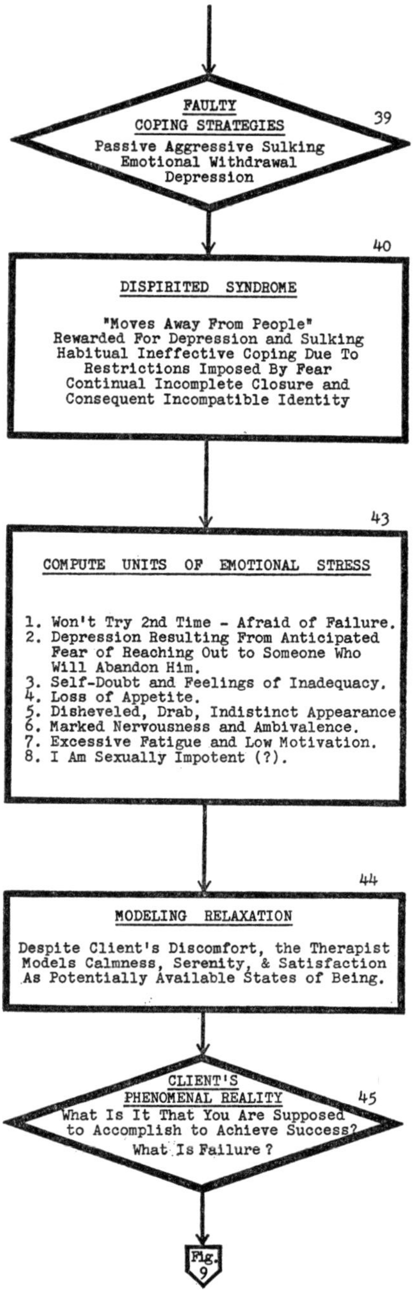

FAULTY
COPING STRATEGIES   39
Passive Aggressive Sulking
Emotional Withdrawal
Depression

                                      40

DISPIRITED SYNDROME

"Moves Away From People"
Rewarded For Depression and Sulking
Habitual Ineffective Coping Due To
Restrictions Imposed By Fear
Continual Incomplete Closure and
Consequent Incompatible Identity

                                      43

COMPUTE UNITS OF EMOTIONAL STRESS

1. Won't Try 2nd Time - Afraid of Failure.
2. Depression Resulting From Anticipated
   Fear of Reaching Out to Someone Who
   Will Abandon Him.
3. Self-Doubt and Feelings of Inadequacy.
4. Loss of Appetite.
5. Disheveled, Drab, Indistinct Appearance.
6. Marked Nervousness and Ambivalence.
7. Excessive Fatigue and Low Motivation.
8. I Am Sexually Impotent (?).

                                      44

MODELING RELAXATION

Despite Client's Discomfort, the Therapist
Models Calmness, Serenity, & Satisfaction
As Potentially Available States of Being.

CLIENT'S
PHENOMENAL REALITY   45
What Is It That You Are Supposed
to Accomplish to Achieve Success?
What Is Failure ?

Fig.
9

Figure 8

Synthesizing what Mat had experienced, it might be said that, as a child, he learned through search and self-discovery. The search was encouraged by his desire to understand how the world around him related to his own individual world. As he grew older, his experiences dictated, to a degree, what course of action he should follow. Some of his understandings were factual and were based on reality. Others were based on fiction, fantasy, and anticipation. When he made a choice, he would go through a sequence of steps including, but not restricted to, such things as circumspection, preemption, and commitment. In reality, however, he could not be circumspect because his understandings were faulty and, therefore, would not stand up to reality testing. His method of preemption was inaccurate because he was not circumspect, *i.e.* he could not select an appropriate alternative because his entire process of reasoning was confused. Finally, most of his commitments ended in failure because he was not circumspect and, therefore, could not work out a logical method of discovering his alternative choices.

THE NEXUS THERAPIST IN ACTION

Actually, Mat could have taken a number of different directions. His movement as a client, therefore, depended to a great extent on the philosophy of the therapist and the techniques he employed as a result of that philosophy. Some therapists might have elected to remain silent during his initial statement. Others might have proceeded from a different theoretical frame of reference and introduced initial statements which were different. No matter how much agreement or disagreement there is among therapists, there is always a basic uniqueness about how each relates with his respective client. This uniqueness is the art by which the therapist internalizes his own relationships. It is the sensitivity by which he is encouraged to employ his techniques and by which he is frequently inspired to change from one technique to another.

It seems apparent that one response to Mat's initial statement of failure could have been, "Oh, come on, Mat; we know you can do it" or "We've got confidence in you, Mat." Such statements, while they might appear feasible, seem to ignore Mat's plea for help. They are, as a matter of fact, statements which could have threatened Mat, for they might well have implied that his therapist had more faith in Mat than he had in himself. He may have had some reservations about whether or not he could live up to such expectations. The threat of failure could then have compounded his problem for he would have been failing his therapist.

Another response might have been, "Everything will be fine." It appears that, if a therapist responded in this way, he would have to be measuring these experiences in terms of his own ability to respond and, thus, ignoring the justifiable fears of his client. Yet, if the therapist says nothing or simply responds by saying, "uh-huh," it seems that he could leave the impression that he does not understand Mat's confusion or that he chose, for some reason, simply to ignore it.

If the therapist elects to respond, it appears that he must take from what Mat said those things which are pertinent. Although anticipating a client is not always a favorite approach to therapy, some therapists might have responded to Mat by saying, "It seems like what you're saying is that you'd like to try again but that there are also reasons for hesitating." The therapist might then pause and, if there is no response, follow with, "Maybe what you're really telling me is that you would like life a lot more if you knew you could find some success" If the person responds with, "Yeah, that's it," then he is on the right track. If not, he can try something else.

Because much of what is done in nexus psychotherapy is based on the notion of intentionality (Misiak and Sexton, 1973), the therapist tries to avoid "feeding" clients. He avoids asking questions and then answering them or structuring the response repertoire and anticipating responses. More specifically, he tries to avoid saying things like, "How do you feel—guilty—apprehensive —shy?" or "It seems like what you're saying is that you'd like to try again but that there are reasons for hesitating," *i.e.* nexus therapists avoid asking and answering their own questions or anticipating a client. They do this simply because such a response may have nothing to do with the client's thoughts. A client may respond to

his therapist's suggestions, because it is easier to respond to someone else's thinking. To avoid this, it seems that one must believe
that the client is the only one who has the necessary understandings to get at the things through an examination of his own con-
sciousness. The therapist or counselor is simply there to help him
explore some methods of bringing those understandings into his
total system of functioning.

Mat's therapy was designed to make him define those things he
was talking about. Even though the definitions are his, the techniques for helping him to discover himself are those of the therapist. This is why therapy is so important to people who need help.
A person normally has difficulty remaining objective enough to go
through a process of self-examination. Unlike education, therapy
is not a self-developing process but implies help from without,
from someone who is trained to accomplish this end. Naturally,
there were other directions that Mat could have taken. Had he
taken a different course of action, the therapist would have responded to that difference. The difference would have been more
a reflection of art than of science. It is important to note this
difference because what a therapist does is inseparable from what
he is, and whatever a client does determines how and to what extent the therapist will respond.

THE APPLICATION OF TREATMENT TECHNIQUES

Up to this point, we know the following things about Mat:
When he applied for nexus therapy, he was a thirty-six-year-old
male and was married. Until he was five, his mother dressed him
like a little girl. When his mother spent more time with his
sister than she did with him, he felt abandoned. He eventually
became very attached to his sister and, at one time, attempted to
use her love as a substitute for his mother's love. As he and his
sister grew older, he made sexual advances toward his sister, which
his father immediately discouraged. When his sister started dating
and especially after she married, he again felt abandoned. His
father died when he was in his late teens and he formed a strong
relationship with his uncle. When he applied for nexus therapy,
he had been under psychiatric care for sixteen years. He experi-

mented with drugs for several years and, on five different occasions, attempted suicide. His appearance, when he first came to therapy was drab and indistinct, and his attitude was one of futility and despair. He had mixed feelings about his wife; at one time, he tried to make her into a prostitute. Several months after therapy had been initiated, however, he wanted her to have more self-respect. He sometimes talked about how he felt drawn to unknown women. It seemed that he felt he would be abandoned by his wife as he was by his mother and his sister.

During his eighth session with his nexus therapist, Mat said several things which permitted his therapist to exercise a press technique, thus challenging Mat to think about some of his values from a different point of view. The following are segments from a transcript of that session and illustrate the use of both perceptual chipping and juxtaposition in assisting the client to develop a more realistic point of view.

Mat began the session by telling his therapist that his wife received a letter from her mother telling her about the loneliness of her life. His wife seemed somewhat depressed by the contents of the letter and shared her feelings with Mat. Mat, in turn, became rather despondent about death and old age and shared his feelings with the therapist. The therapist took this opportunity to help Mat reexamine the polarity of his relationship with his wife and what purpose such polarity would serve.

TRANSCRIPT SEGMENTS

M = Mat
T = Therapist

M: With my wife, I don't think it's so much a fear of death as the fear of somebody else dying — somebody that she loved — you know.

T: Maybe.

M: I've started trying to pay more attention to her — to do more things with her, and this seems to make her feel better. You know, I look at other girls a lot, and I think she gets jealous because I don't look at her that much.

T: I wonder why you'd do that.

M: I don't know.

T: It's almost like you're trying to find something that you
        dont have. (pause)

NOTE: The therapist is now beginning to move Mat toward the
        reality of the separatism he has practiced for so long in
        his marriage. He believes that Mat learned to polarize
        relationships after his experience with his mother. He
        further believes that the relationship with his sister re-
        inforced his need to remain at a distance and that his
        wife, in many respects, is the victim of his faulty percep-
        tion.

T: And still she's a good partner — a good mate and a good
        sexual partner.

M: Uh-huh. — But ah, I think part of it, the physical attrac-
        tion, is — ah, the girl that I love I'm not as physically at-
        tracted to as I am to other girls.

NOTE: The therapist now begins his press by utilizing percep-
        tual chipping and juxtaposition.

T: Were you physically attracted to your wife when you first
        married her?

M: Yeah — uh-huh — yeah.

T: Were you physically attracted to her when you got mar-
        ried to her?

M: Yeah — Yeah, I think so. Maybe just as the physical at-
        tractiveness was starting to decline — I think. Ah,
        another thing about physical attraction is that she
        doesn't have that much self-respect. She doesn't have
        good feelings about herself.

T: Uh-huh — but you wouldn't know how much self-respect
        a stranger has, would you? If you saw a stranger, a
        woman walking down the street, you wouldn't know if
        she was what you wanted — if she had self respect — if
        she had good feelings about herself, would you?

M: Uh Uh.

T: So that may not be why you're looking at other women.

M: But — but how do I get her to have more self-respect?

T: Well, what have you done in the relationship that
        causes her to respond the way she does now?

NOTE: The therapist begins his move to juxtapose the request
        of his client against the reality of his client's actions.

M: I don't know.

T: How about those months you spent getting her to dress and act like a whore?

M: What can I do? How can I get her to have more self-respect?

NOTE: The therapist now assumes that the client is ready for a Type II experience and offers some guidelines.

T: By treating her like she's a worthy person.

M: By having more patience with her?

T: Well, you use patience like it's something you have to do mechanically.

M: Unh.

T: I'm saying, how honest are you in the relationship?

M: How honest?

T: Yeah — If you have to have patience with someone, it doesn't seem that you're very honest. It implies that you're frustrated and that you have to control yourself in some forced way in order to tolerate the person. I'm asking you what's happening in the relationship and why is it happening? (pause)

M: Uh-huh.

T: The other thing is that those girls you see — that you find physically attractive before you even know them — isn't part of that physical attraction in your mind? Isn't that part of the fantasy that we talked about? (pause)

NOTE: The client was classified as schizophrenic and originally experienced delusions and hallucinations which were frequently referred to as fantasies.

T: — the idea that a girl can be anything that you want. You don't want to deal with what she is, so she becomes what you want. With your wife, you're dealing with reality — what she is.

M: Yeah — uh-huh.

T: So, if you want to masturbate over the concept of the "fantasy girl" or whatever — then you can do this and she can be anything you want.

NOTE: The client has had a long history of masturbation and originally applied for therapy saying he was impotent. When asked what that meant, he said that, although he had sexual relations with his wife and she reached orgasm, he never did. This he felt was a sign of impotence. He also said that he frequently selected pictures of girls from magazines and then masturbated while looking at those pictures.

M: Yeah — uh-huh

T: But that's not what she really is — it's what you make her.

M: Uh-huh.

T: But that's not what she really is. (pause) At the same time, you almost ignore what your wife is.

M: Yeah (pause).

T: Instead of finding out what she really is in the relationship — letting yourself go instead of holding yourself apart from that relationship. This is essentially what you're doing, isn't it?

NOTE: The therapist moves him closer to understanding the impact of abandonment and how his relationship with his mother has served as a construct for his relationship with his wife.

T: You're practicing separatism in your relationship with your wife, aren't you? You're practicing depersonalization with her; otherwise, you wouldn't be looking at other girls all the time and using pictures of girls the way you do. It's like you don't want to get too close to your wife because you don't want to fall in love with her. What will happen? Will she abandon you like your mother and your sister? Is that what this is all about?

M: If I get to close to her — uh-huh. Yeah, there's nothing wrong with looking at other girls, but with me — I don't know, I've grown in love with my wife to a certain extent but — I, ah, stopped there. We haven't progressed. We haven't gotten any closer.

T: Well, you can get as close as you want to get.

M: One of the things I've started doing is expressing my feelings more — if she makes me angry, I express myself more. Before, I worried about her getting upset.

T: Getting angry and remaining silent about it, isn't that a way of practicing separatism with your wife also? And, impotence when she wants a sexual relationship, isn't that a way of practicing separatism?

M: Yeah — uh-huh —

T: I wonder why you'd be doing that.

M: It's like — ah, I got into an argument with her this week downtown. Which is the first time we've ever done that — let off steam. But before, I've been afraid to do that because I was afraid she'd leave me.

NOTE: It is interesting to note that, while he agrees that he fears abandonment, he has also reached a new level in assertiveness. At this point, he asserts himself with his wife and poses a threat to the relationship. The therapist moves to close this gap between the client's ability to relate to his wife and his ability to find expression within that relationship.

T: Well, what are you saying now, that you want her to leave?

M: No — I've been trying to — ah, I can't hold back some of these feelings.

T: You shouldn't hold them back, but I'm asking you what those feelings are. What are you doing in the relationship that causes her to respond so that you become frustrated?

M: Holding back negative feelings toward her — not expressing them.

T: Yeah, but why should you have negative feelings toward her?

M: Well, I'm beginning to have both negative and positive feelings.

T: I don't understand. What's she doing and what are you doing?

M: I don't know.

T: Well, what's happening? Tell me about your relationship.

M: We've been having arguments.

T: Tell me about them.

M: Well, usually she complained about something — got angry — complained about something.

T: She complained about something — now don't just tell me she complained about something, tell me what she complained about.

M: (pause) Well let me see, I've forgotten now — well,

about the way things are going.

T: How are they going?

M: Well, I always thought they were going the same — you know.

T: Yeah, well, I don't know what that means, either.

M: Well, the main thing she complained about was my spending too much money. You know — I'm getting short — I went to the doctors Saturday — we argued over that.

NOTE: Mat went to the doctor after his sixth session because he became violently ill after discussing with his therapist the sexual advances he made toward his sister and the immediate retaliation by his father. His wife felt he was not really sick. The doctor seemed to confirm this. The therapist dealt with this during the seventh session, but it had not been discussed during this session, his eighth.

M: We're getting low on money now. We had to borrow some recently; I'm getting a loan. I don't have it yet, but I'm getting it. That's one thing, there are other things. But she doesn't come out and say what they are. They're hints — sometimes she tells me.

T: How do you respond to that?

M: I try to do better — but I got angry back.

T: What did you say?

M: That she shouldn't get worried about it or something like that.

T: Or something like that.

M: Yeah.

T: How did you say it?

M: Well, I said we'll figure out something (pause).

T: Is that the way you said it — in a very soft tone — the way you just said it to me?

M: No — I was more angry. She started crying a little bit — just a little bit. Then she said I wasn't paying enough attention to her.

T: What do you think that really means?

M: Not paying enough attention to her?

T: Yeah.

M: I think she realizes that I'm more excited by a whore than I am her.

T: All right, so essentially what you are saying is that she realizes that you're not paying very much attention to her physically.

M: That's right.

T: Now you're aware of it, and she's aware of it.

M: Yeah.

T: Well, what are you going to do about it?

M: Well, I've been working on it. What I've been working on is not having these fantasies anymore. But the problem is I have difficulty when she doesn't have self-respect.

T: I'm not sure what that means.

M: I'm not sure either. I know that I can get aroused by another girl if she has self-respect.

T: You're talking around something and I don't really understand what it is. This must have some sexual connotations — self-respect. What is it she should be doing in a sexual relationship with you that reflects self-respect?

M: That she has self-respect.

T: Yeah, what is it she should be doing?

M: Standing up for her rights, I guess.

T: In her relationship with you?

M: Yeah — un-huh.

T: What are her rights?

M: She's an individual in and by herself.

T: Yeah and what is it you think your doing to her that you think you shouldn't be doing to her?

M: I have the feeling that, in the past, I've been making her into a sex object (pause) a whore.

T: Well, why don't you tell her so that she understands?

M: Tell her that I've been doing that?

T: Tell her that you don't want to do it — that you want to respect her (pause) so that she understands.

M: Uh-huh.

T: All these months you've been trying to change her into something else; now, all of a sudden, you don't respect what you've done.

M: Yeah — that's what it is.

T: Well, maybe you're changing.

M: Yeah, not only with my wife, but I notice when I masturbate, I'm having trouble imagining the girl.

T: What do you think that means?

M: I don't know. I think I do things I did in the past, but that they don't have the same meaning. I'm changing — but I — if, if I — my feelings for my wife change and — what will happen to me.

T: I don't know, Mat, what will happen?

M: That's it, I don't know (pause) maybe our relationship will get better.

T: And if it doesn't?

M: Well, then it will be like it is — but I don't think that will happen. She wants me to love her, ah — pay more attention to her.

T: Then why don't you do that?

M: Well, I guess I — what I have to do is find out — what our relationship is like. I just have to do it.

T: Can you come back on Friday?

M: Uh-huh.

SCHEMATIC INTERPRETATION

A partial schematic depicting Type II problem therapeutic intervention based on Mat's eighth session is presented in Figures 9 and 10.

PATTERN FORMATION

Some years ago, Karen Horney (1942) listed ten interpersonal patterns or neurotic trends which children might develop. In a way, these trends were really clusters of responses directed toward adults by children as they attempted to sustain themselves. Basically, she felt that children moved in three ways: toward people, against people, or away from people. Apparently, she felt they did this in a search for security.

Applying this understanding to Mat's case, it appears that he first attempted to move toward his mother. When this did not work, he obviously moved away from her and became an isolate. He followed somewhat of an avoidance pattern and this, in turn, seemed to help him to get some attention.

To this extent Mat's life was greatly influenced by his relationship with his mother. Unfortunately the pattern Mat followed became the essence of his depression not only because it did not

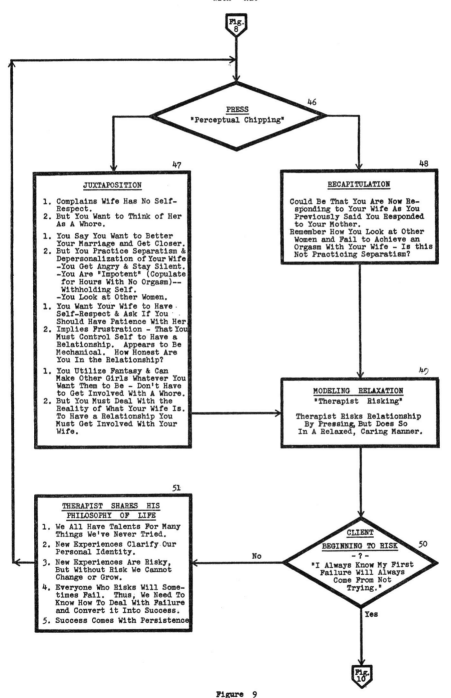

Fig. 8

PRESS
"Perceptual Chipping"   46

JUXTAPOSITION   47

1. Complains Wife Has No Self-Respect.
2. But You Want to Think of Her As A Whore.

1. You Say You Want to Better Your Marriage and Get Closer.
2. But You Practice Separatism & Depersonalization of Your Wife
   -You Get Angry & Stay Silent.
   -You Are "Impotent" (Copulate for Hours With No Orgasm)--Withholding Self.
   -You Look at Other Women.

1. You Want Your Wife to Have Self-Respect & Ask If You Should Have Patience With Her.
2. Implies Frustration - That You Must Control Self to Have a Relationship. Appears to Be Mechanical. How Honest Are You In the Relationship?

1. You Utilize Fantasy & Can Make Other Girls Whatever You Want Them to Be - Don't Have to Get Involved With A Whore.
2. But You Must Deal With the Reality of What Your Wife Is. To Have a Relationship You Must Get Involved With Your Wife.

RECAPITULATION   48

Could Be That You Are Now Responding to Your Wife As You Previously Said You Responded to Your Mother.
Remember How You Look at Other Women and Fail to Achieve an Orgasm With Your Wife - Is this Not Practicing Separatism?

MODELING RELAXATION   49
"Therapist Risking"

Therapist Risks Relationship By Pressing, But Does So In A Relaxed, Caring Manner.

THERAPIST SHARES HIS PHILOSOPHY OF LIFE   51

1. We All Have Talents For Many Things We've Never Tried.
2. New Experiences Clarify Our Personal Identity.
3. New Experiences Are Risky, But Without Risk We Cannot Change or Grow.
4. Everyone Who Risks Will Sometimes Fail. Thus, We Need To Know How To Deal With Failure and Convert it Into Success.
5. Success Comes With Persistence.

CLIENT
BEGINNING TO RISK   50
- ? -
"I Always Know My First Failure Will Always Come From Not Trying."

No

Yes

Fig. 10

Figure 9

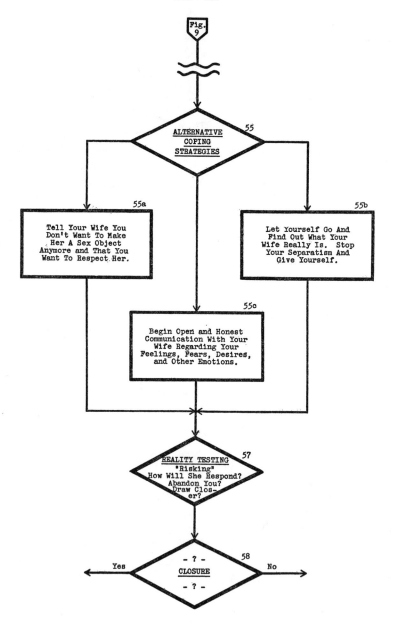

Figure 10

work once he became an adult but because he did not understand how to change the pattern so that it would work. Becoming an isolate as Mat did meant that he had to find his identity through others. Yet each time he did that he sacrificed his own identity. He permitted others to make his decisions so that he could avoid the pain of failure. Yet, to do this reinforced his depression because he could never become his own person. It seems that, each time Mat moved, he sought closure, *i.e.* the ability to bring his experiences into harmony with his total system of functioning. The relationship with his mother failed to provide such closure, so he went to his sister. Because neither his mother nor his sister realized what he wanted, they responded to him in terms of his neurotic moods. His reaction to their presence was simply a repetition of what he had done as a child, and to that extent, he remained a child until he entered into therapy.

CHAPTER 6

NEXUS PSYCHOTHERAPY: OTHER MOVEMENTS AND COPING STRATEGIES

M AT'S MOVEMENT AWAY from people was learned as an anticipa-
tory experience which occurred when he could not gain his
mother's attention. Because the attitude he formed as a result of
that frustrating experience caused in him a mood to which his
mother responded, he continued to call upon the mood whenever
he wanted more attention. In his later life, he generalized this
mood to each situation in which he felt insecure. Gradually, it
became part of almost every experience he had, simply because
when he was moody and withdrawn, people were attentive. The
attention, however, was not very fulfilling, for it caused him to
sacrifice his personal identity in an effort to gain what, at best,
was a poor relationship based on self-despair.

Karen Horney (1942), however, suggested that there were
other movements a person could make: One was to move against
people; the other was to move toward people.

THE CASE OF DENNY

To illustrate, by contrast, how a client functions when he
moves against people, we have selected the case of Denny. Denny
was extremely critical. After listening to the way he condemned
his parents, one might even say that he was abusive. He described
his father as a "rotten" alcoholic, who had no interest in him, and
his mother as a "freak" neurotic, without love for anyone.

Denny had been under psychiatric care for a number of years.
Actually, his first experience with a psychiatrist came at a very
early age. Later, he returned for psychiatric care because the
drugs he got from his doctor "turned him on." In the best in-

112

terests of psychiatry, however, it should be noted that this attack on his psychiatrist seemed a natural part of his hypercritical and extremely agressive attitude toward everyone.

As an adult, his sophisticated medical language carried with it the telltale signs of his relationship with psychiatrists. When he originally requested nexus therapy, he identified himself as a paranoid-schizophrenic with sociopathic tendencies. He seemed to find some satisfaction in having such a distinctive title but admitted that the only reason he came was because he no longer had the funds to continue psychiatric care. Denny, at that point in his life, was a rootless person. He was twenty-one years old, tall, thin, and rather emaciated. His hair was long and disheveled. For some reason, it always looked like it was washed with glue. To offset this totally unkempt, look, he wore small gold-rimmed glasses and peculiarly oversized clothes.

Despite his constant griping, Denny was really an intertesting person. At times he seemed warm and sensitive—at other times, aggressive and arrogant.

One of the most impressive things about Denny was the swiftness with which he learned to acknowledge his responsibility in any given relationship. Some therapists would probably interpret this as a reflection of his sociopathic tendencies. Yet, Denny seemed more willing to participate in a process of self-examination than does the typical sociopathic person and seemed especially willing to examine his relationships to determine what he did to cause people to react negatively.

HIS FEAR OF THE FUTURE. It was obvious that Denny was a rigid person and that much of his rigidity grew out of his concern for himself and his fear of the future. One of his main concerns was trying to define his relationship with his parents. He constantly struggled for a relationship with his family which would give him the feeling of completeness and worth that he wanted. Over the years, Denny had become a truly fine musician, but he felt that his parents ignored his talent. Obviously, the members of his family were engaged in an extremely painful battle of life which, at best, seemed destined to destroy all of them. His only solace was his music. As a musician, he was magnificent. There was nothing in the world of music which seemed beyond his reach. Yet, his musical success never brought complete fulfillment. Music seemed to be no more than a catharsis, a way of channeling his expressive feelings without becoming involved with people. Once he found that he could use music in this way, it became his crutch. In essence, what everyone heard from Denny was always in code—if a person could not interpret from his music what Denny was communicating, then he never really knew him. This is one of the interesting things about art; therapists have long appreciated the fact that one can communicate through art and release a great deal of feeling. After studying artists receiving therapy, it now seems that communicating in this way could very easily lead to a deficiency in communicating in other ways. With Denny, music was a safety valve. He never had to deal with his feelings directly because music gave him just enough release so that he could survive for one more day.

RIGIDITY AS A COPING STRATEGY. Characteristically, Denny wanted to do things to perfection. He was meticulous, methodical, and exacting about his music, as well as many other facets of his life. Most of the time, it seemed that his structuring provided protection against failure When he used such structuring in his own life, he appeared to be endowed with excellence. It was as he imposed this structure on those around him that life became sheer hell. In many respects, Denny was irreversible, unyielding, and hypercritical about how one should perform musically. He developed this method of coping because he was unsure of himself. This was his way of coping with failure; "Ya gotta be good," he once said, "So good that no one can ever challenge you." He worried constantly about trifles—little things that might happen to him. Sometimes he became submissive simply to gain the control he needed in order to move in the direction of his choice. In many respects, he was relentless and forced his ideas upon others; in other respects, he seemed almost passive. Yet, deep inside, he appeared always to be a seething mass of hostility.

When what he did was less than perfect, he was quick to shift the blame for imperfection to others. In this respect, he was constantly projecting. He frequently supported his own actions by criticizing the actions of others who worked with him.

At times, nothing he did seemed to give him a sense of security. When he felt this way, he would go to a therapist. It was at such a moment that we first met him. In a sense, Denny was the attacker. He intruded himself into the world around him with the energy of an angry bull. Most of the time, he expected the world around him to change. By intimidating the musicians who worked for him, he played the game of life by his rules. Unfortunately, musical success never seemed to bring fulfillment. Although he wanted more out of life, his actions created situations that resulted in less. Even his fellow musicians regarded him as "strange."

HIS SORDID PAST. When he did not have his music as a release, he became unmercifully critical. One of his fellow musicians once said of him, "He has a personality like sandpaper and disposition to match it." Once in this mood, no human within reach went untouched by his vindictiveness. He crucified his parents with the prolific sophistication of Satan doing battle with the Lord. Yet, at other times, he became very quiet and seemed at those moments to be in a state of meditation. Obviously, his style of living, his sexual promiscuity, his drug abuse, and his general appearance all seemed to conflict with his well-disciplined approach to music.

At one point in his life, he even joined a zealous religious cult. He wanted peace, he said. At first, he thought that religion might be the answer. The frustrations he experienced, however, soon drove him back to drugs. It was while he was with one of his friends, a former addict, that he was encouraged to try therapy once again.

HIS GROUP EXPERIENCES. During his initial relationship with his nexus therapist, Denny told him of his group experiences and how two people in the group said things that made him terribly uncomfortable. He told him,

> Two people brought up some things that have been brought up to me before. One guy said I don't listen (pause). He said I didn't seem concerned about anyone. One girl said if she wanted to talk to someone about some difficulty, I'd be the last one she'd talk to, (pause) and then the group goes "uh-huh" — all nodding their heads. It wasn't really news to me.

His therapist responded with, "You've had this type of feed-back before."

Yeah, yeah, lots of times, and I try to look concerned, but I'm not. I try to tell them that I don't like any of them — that I don't like anyone, including myself and that they didn't help me figure that out. The group is dead. They don't care about anything — they don't care much about me, and like I said, I don't much care about anybody. The whole thing seems hopeless. Nobody seems to care much about me — which doesn't bother me — some-times — but a lot of times, it does."

HIS SEARCH FOR IDENTITY. In reality, Denny seemed to be searching for personal identity. He tried to find it through drugs, music, religious cults, alcohol, and sex. Unfortunately, he failed to search deep within himself. When he failed to find something in life which was meaningful, he became frustrated, hostile, and aggressive. He looked at his failures in life and blamed his parents, peers, or anyone else who was readily available. His group experiences had been traumatic because of the verbal attack launched against him, and his sexual relationship with his girl friend had recently terminated because of a violent argument. All these conflicts made him feel alone, rootless, and without identity. The futility of his life made him wonder whether or not he should go on. At times he felt suicidal. Yet, during his most distressing moments, his strength of character and his well-disci-plined mind gave him hope for a better future. His therapy was a means of reaffirming that hope.

The beauty of his relationship with his therapist was reflected when Denny said, "The whole thing seems hopeless. Nobody seems to care much about me—which doesn't bother me—some-times—but a lot of times, it does."

It must have taken a great deal of courage for Denny to make that statement. This is a statement made by a person who re-portedly never cared about anyone. Yet, at this moment he ad-mitted that he was concerned with the way people felt about him.

There are three things that Denny has told us up to this point. First, it seems obvious from his conversations that he is highly critical of people. This is probably an extension of his own personal desire to be meticulous and to intrude his values into the lives of others. Second, he is extremely frustrated. It appears that his meticulousness does not work as a coping strategy, and that, as a result, he does not relate well with people. Third, he is experiencing some depression because he does not know how to find a better way of relating. This probably means that he has reached a point where his choice of alternative courses of action seems limited or may even be exhausted. Denny's Primary Learning Route, which essentially is that of the Rigid Syndrome, is depicted in Figure 11.

The responsibility of his therapist is to help him reach a level of thinking which will bring with it the potential for new attitudes. That is, his therapist must help Denny to reach a point in his thinking where he recognizes that certain experiences in his life have been misinterpreted, and that, through reexamination, these experiences could change. To accomplish this end, one press technique employed was perceptual chipping. Because Denny was a self-proclaimed "miserable, wretched character who never experienced happiness and who cried a lot because of it," it was simple to press Denny in this area. Obviously, he found some comfort in the idea that he was a hopeless product of his environment because it made someone else or something else responsible for the miserable wretch he was. Yet, it also seemed that, by confiding in his nexus therapist this way, he might be attempting to avoid his therapist's personal interpretation of him as a human being. To that extent, he may have disarmed his previous therapists. That is, if a client or parent tells you how bad he is, what is there left to be evaluated?

His Self-Hate. When his therapist asked what this self-hate was like, he responded by saying,

I feel that I'm inferior to everyone and everything. (pause) I hate college — I hate the prospects of (pause) . . . I hate my plans for life — my future — what I'm going to do. I hate my girl. I hate my life. I hate driving my car. I hate getting up in the morning. I hate going to bed at night. How's that? (pause) I hate my life. I'd like to end it. I'm such a chicken I'd never do it. (pause)

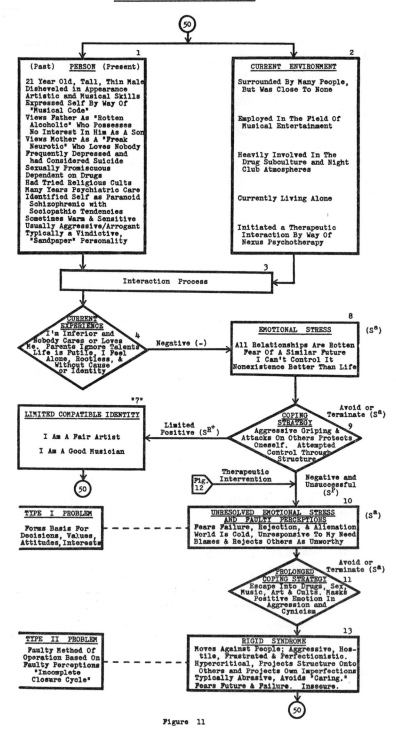

Figure 11

I have no religion, so I have no heaven or hell to look forward to. I have no self-respect. A person has to — has to like himself a little bit. I don't like myself at all.

His therapist's perceptual chiping started with, "There's nothing about yourself that you like?

Well, I'm a pretty fair artist and a good musician, but that's all — whatever that means — you know? I have no pride in that. That's — those are the only things about me that I'd want anybody to know about. That doesn't mean anything. You know what I mean?

"I'm not sure," said the therapist.

Well, a guy comes up to me and says, "Hey, man, I'd really like to have that painting. How much do you want for it?" and I say, $80 — then the guy says, "How about $10?" Then we dicker for awhile, and he says, "I'll come back when I get the bread." But he won't — you know? It's bad. 'Course, everybody thinks art is nothing — anybody can do it. It's like music.

I suppose I should tell you that four years ago I started seeing Dr. T . . . in J . . . . He's a psychiatrist — you know? Well, what I thought was a miracle happened to me. He put me on medication — and, ah (pause) then I felt great — really great. But it lasted for only a short time. I'm — ah, rambling now.

I've been going down, down, down. I hate my girl friend — things are bad between us. Sue (his girl friend) was having some emotional difficulties, and I helped her out — and, ah, she admits that. But now she's my crutch. And I did drugs, then religion — now Sue is my crutch. Well, not really — she dumped me. It's a dependency. I can't rely on myself. And that means I have to find something to rely on. Drugs are bad news — ah, religion is bad news, and, ah — sex is okay if you can have it whenever you want it.

The therapist responded by asking, "What is this crutch you keep talking about?"

One of my problems is that, when I get really lonely, I start freaking out. When there's nobody around — I get "spooked" — I go to Sue. I keep her around for companionship. I need her. (pause) I hate myself for that — needing people. I want to feel

content and happy.   There are things I should be doing for myself.
You probably think I haven't tried hard enough.   Well, I guarantee you I've tried.   (pause) I've tried everything — everything.

The therapist said, "It seems that Denny can't do it by himself.
He needs help."

Yeah, it's easier to let God do it, or Sue do it, or drugs do it.   But
I'm sure I can't do it by myself. (pause)
I'm sure that it all goes back to my family.   My parents are disin-
terested.   That's where my earlier problems stem from—I'm sure.
My parents were never really parents — you know?   The "old
man" never played ball with me — never came to see me perform
(as a musician), never.   And, ah — my mother was nothing —
you know?   She was there to tell me to wash my clothes and stuff
like that, but emotionally, she never mothered me.   You know
what I mean?   (pause).
"I guess you're saying you wanted more from her," said the therapist.
Yeah, well — I wanted her to love me for one thing.   I wanted
her to protect me — you know — when I was a kid.   I ah — ah —
realized that I'm messed up and that things are getting worse.
"Worse," said the therapist.
Yeah, I have a high level of anxiety — and, ah, I find myself
doing strange things.
"I'm not sure I understand," said the therapist.
Well, like dropping acid, smoking pot, and then doing freaky
things.
"Freaky — huh?" responded the therapist.
Yeah, you know?   Like I leave this world, but I don't know
where my body is.   I get this strange kind of happiness — elation
maybe.
"But only on drugs, huh? Happiness is drugs." said the thera-
pist.
Yeah, but ah — no, not always on drugs.
"Sometimes happiness can be something else — something other
than drugs," said the therapist.

Yeah, like if I do a show — then after the show, I pack my horn and go home — then go to bed — ah, then sometimes when I wake up the next morning, I feel really great. But then when I get ready for the next show — it's bad. I can hardly describe how bad it is. (pause) It's hard to describe. I just about die.

"I wonder what that is?" asked the therapist, "that feeling that you get the next morning."

I don't know.

"But it's possible for you to feel happy without drugs — to feel good," said the therapist.

Yeah, and it will come again after I'm finished playing. But now, man — before I go on, it's rough . I'm dying all over the place.

"I wonder what that means?" asked the therapist.

Dr. T . . . . . said it was fear. (pause)

"It seems you have some reservations about that," said the therapist.

Yeah, maybe it's fear, but I have no thoughst about my playing. The only thing that might cause some difficulty would be the cold. If it's cold, I might not hit some of the high notes — but this really doesn't bother me. It never has, and it never will. It's kind of hard to put my finger on it. When he told me that (reference to Dr. T . . . . .) , I thought about it but when I'm playing, nothing bothers me. I never worry about failure — maybe I worry about doing the best I can or about being sure I have all the music or — I just don't know. What he said really doesn't seem to fit. (pause) Is — ah — is my life going to be like this forever?

"You seem to feel that there must be more," said the therapist.

I suppose that, at best, I would like each day to be like the morning after a performance. At worst, my life is without hope. Ah — I'm not going to tell you that I'll commit suicide 'cause I tried — I started to do it, but — well it's no longer in my mind but — I can't tell you that burning in a Christian hell wouldn't almost be better than this — my only hope is death and — ah, maybe a complete nothingness.

His Insights. Before Denny could assert himself, he had to understand the reality of what it was he feared. Thus, in our relationship, there was a great deal of perceptual chipping. He had to examine and reexamine the accuracy of what he experienced. When he said, "My parents were never really parents—you know?" it seemed that he would first have to determine what he wanted from the relationship, and then compare it with what he actually got. Naturally, as he did this, he also had to determine how well he communicated within the relationship.

Several weeks later, he once again pursued this hate theme. He said, "I guess most of what I am I can blame on my parents— you know? They were never really parents."

To which his therapist responded, "And still it seems that they did what they could—you're an excellent artist and an accomplished musician." "Yeah, yeah—they did that." He paused for a long time and then said,

I — I — ah, don't often think about what they've done — mostly what they haven't. (pause) Boy, you really zapped me. (pause) I guess what you're telling me is that I'm looking through the wrong end of the tube. Sometimes, I think about how come I don't love — love! Ha! That's — that's really a strange word. But sometimes, I think about how come I don't even — even like. (pause).

"You mean love," said the therapist.

Yeah, love my parents, and I think I must be some kind of kook.

"Perhaps they've expressed their love in the only ways they know how — in ways you didn't always understand," said the therapist.

Yeah — yeah — they have. It's true they never come to see me perform, but they helped me buy my first instrument.

"And maybe helped pay for lessons," said the therapist.

Yeah, that's true. But my mother — she raised hell with me — nothing was ever right. But I, ah — maybe she didn't want me to be a booze freak like my old man. And look what she got. I've done it all. Yeah, that's good. It's a good thought — something I can live with. I like that. Maybe both of them were trying but just couldn't pull it off. Huh — yeah — it's like I'm just beginning to understand that maybe they liked me but maybe — ah — maybe, like me, didn't — or, ah, couldn't show it. It's like love — God it's hard for me to say that — that word — it makes me feel weak or — ashamed — or — I don't know what the hell it makes me feel. I just can't seem to use the word. That is — ah — with — any comfort.

"Maybe you're using the word rather than feeling it," said the therapist.

You mean like it, it's — ah — detached — not really part of me, and then I use it mechanically. Then I don't feel comfortable with it. (pause) Yeah, it's like lying to yourself — you know — trying to say something that's not really you.

Each time Denny was confronted with an attitudinal chip, he seemed to reevaluate the situation in which he found himself and to move toward a more flexible position. In each of these situations, he became more tolerant of others. Naturally, this took place over a longer period of time than is evident by the typescript. Therefore, he had the opportunity to reality test many of the changes he felt he would make before they became final. This segment of nexus intervention is partially displayed in Figure 12.

Denny, like Mat, seemed to respond to a form of "counterchipping" by which old attitudes are challenged and eventually displaced by new attitudes. This, however, is not the only type of perceptual chipping which takes place. Some years ago, Medard Boss (1961) introduced the case of Dr. Cobling, a woman who was medical director of the institution in which they worked. She discussed with him the far-reaching consequences of a fantasized invasion of the earth. Because of her medical sophistication, he found that conventional therapy did not work and eventually restored to what he called *Daseinsanalysis*. In practice, this is a therapeutic approach to relating which is governed by the existential disposition of the patient. Finding himself without any real basis from which to work, Boss finally decided to treat the fantasy as a reality—since, to her, it was a reality. He recognized, perhaps for the first time that as a psychiatrist he had to look at the patient herself and not necessarily the psycho-physiological imbalance that may or may not exist. Realizing that he could do little to combat the hallucinations of his client with conventional therapy, he simply decided to let them stand as the phenomena they were. By so doing, he entered into a practice of perceptual chipping, for he forced the patient to deal with her hallucinations to the extent that she saw them for what they were. Her return

Segment Of

TYPE I PROBLEM INTERVENTION

With "Denny"

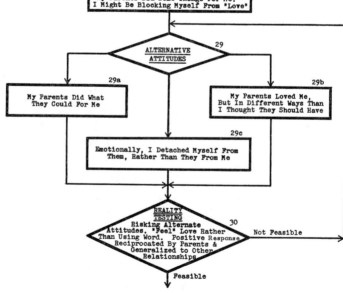

ATTITUDES RECEPTIVE TO CHANGE — 24
Happiness Without Drugs
Rejection or Personal Withdrawal?
Dependency Needs and Fears
Feelings of Self-Worth
What He Desired From Parents
The Meaning of Love and Caring

PRESS — 25
"Perceptual Chipping"

JUXTAPOSITION — 26

1. Most of What I Am I Can Blame on My Parents - They Never Were Good Parents.
2. And Still It Seems They Did What They Could -- You're an Excellent Artist & an Accomplished Musician.

1. My Parents Never Came To See Me Perform.
2. Yet, They Paid For Your Music Lessons.

1. I Am Not Experiencing Love.
2. Maybe Its Because You're Using It Rather Than Feeling It.

RECAPITULATION — 27

1. You've Previously Stated, and You Now Reiterate, There's NOTHING About Yourself That You Like?
2. Well, I'm A Pretty Fair Artist and an Excellent Musician.

CONSEQUENCES — 28
I'm Not Hopeless, or Totally Without Good Qualities.
My Parents Did Some Things For Me.
I Might Be Blocking Myself From "Love"

ALTERNATIVE ATTITUDES — 29

29a My Parents Did What They Could For Me

29b My Parents Loved Me, But In Different Ways Than I Thought They Should Have

29c Emotionally, I Detached Myself From Them, Rather Than They From Me

REALITY TESTING — 30
Risking Alternate Attitudes. "Feel" Love Rather Than Using Word. Positive Response Reciprocated By Parents & Generalized to Other Relationships

Not Feasible

Feasible

Figure 12

to emotional stability was an extension of her ability to learn to deal with all aspects of her life in a rational way. The way of reason, however, was built on self-examination as opposed to an examination by others. Then, too, since the world with which they dealt was her world, she was free to explore it at her convenience. The psychiatrist simply served as a catalyst by bringing her world of hallucinations into proper perspective. He did this by encouraging her to examine the things she was talking about in terms of the reality they had for her.

REALITY TESTING. Philosophically speaking, it seems that parents try, for the most part, to do as much as they can for their children. When they are not doing more, it is perhaps because they feel they can do no more.

Denny's parents were probably much like most parents in this respect. Therefore, it seemed that they were more interested in helping him than hurting him. However, before introducing such ideas into therapeutic conversations with Denny, several precautions seemed essential. First, it was necessary for the therapist to see Denny over a period of time and to develop a relationship which would not falter under such challenges. The basis for that relationship was sensitivity and respect. It involved the ability not only to say the "right" thing but to say it at the "right" time. These are two variables which define, to a great extent, the art of psychotherapy. What it suggests as part of a theoretical premise is that, as you get to know a person, you develop some respect for his moods. Knowing this made it possible for Denny to explore highly sensitive areas when he was relaxed and thoughtful. This sensing process involved both verbal and nonverbal cues. When Denny spoke softly and deliberately, he seemed more capable of change and more receptive to courses of action involving change.

Second, the basis upon which his therapeutic relationship was formed was not predicated on the idea that Denny's values had to be attacked and the therapist's values intruded. Rather, Denny was encouraged to deal with those things he felt were significant and, together with his therapist, ponder his intentions rather than his behavior.

Third, the therapist's presence served as a model within the relationship. If what the therapist reflected was a calm and soothing disposition, then eventually, Denny became a calm and relaxed person.

One of his most successful understandings resulted from Denny's inability to use the word "love." When the therapist said, "Maybe it's because you're using it rather than feeling it," he seemed to understand that he did not know how to love simply because he felt that no one loved him. Obviously, this feeling was based on his personal interpretation of how his parents expressed their love. If they were not expressing love in a way which he easily understood, then he felt that they did not love him.

Through therapy, he was encouraged to reappraise his relationship with his parents and to examine his own detachment in that relationship.* As a result, he formed a new and more meaningful relationship with his parents. To this extent, he tested against reality what he had discovered within his relationship with his therapist. The results, although not entirely what he wanted at first, paved the way for a closer relationship with his parents. Ultimately, he noticed a change in how they responded to him. He reacted to this change quite positively and generalized his positive feelings to other relationships. During the past year, he has grown from a recluse bent on self-destruction to a rather mature young man who is not difficult to like and who continues to grow in his relationships with others.

THE IMPACT OF THE GROUP. One of Denny's problems when he first applied for nexus therapy was that he had been victimized by members of a group. His defeating experiences within the group caused him to think seriously about suicide. It was the massive opposition generated within the group that was so self-defeating to him. He felt that he was alone. Even as he sat in a group with people who were his emotional peers, he was being rejected. The tremendous impact of such an experience was difficult to reverse.

Perhaps what his group facilitator failed to realize was that, once the number of people within a setting is increased, the prob-

---

*Lazarus (1966, 1968) suggested that stimuli that have been appraised as threatening may be reappraised as benign.

lem of relating is automatically compounded. Unfortunately, Denny never got the support he felt a group experience might bring. Fortunately, he did not run away from therapy but was tenacious enough to try again.

MASKING. One of the things that Denny realized was that he frequently masked when he was in a situation which called for some kind of human relationship. In practice, what that meant was that he sometimes became what he felt others wanted him to be. Although he did this with a lot less consistency than did Mat, he did use it as a coping strategy.

Denny sometimes referred to life as a game. His therapist once responded to this comment by saying, "The name of the game is life. If you want to win, you have to play." Philosophically, Denny responded by saying, "And what is it you win?" To which the therapist immediately responded, "The right to participate." He could appreciate that response because he knew from his own experience that he was becoming a more active participant in society. His girl friend was beginning to respond to him quite positively, his parents were responding with what he considered love, and the members of his musical group were beginning to spend a great deal of their personal time with him.

What Denny learned was that, when you mask, you fail to become your own person. As a result, you lose some of your identity and with it the self-expression that makes you a free and psychologically open person. Denny's alternate coping strategies and therapeutic movement toward closure and a more compatible identity are seen in Figure 13.

As he reached a terminal point in therapy, Denny said that he originally thought of masking as a protection against abuse and as an indication of strength. His therapist asked him if he was familiar with Kafka's parable, *Metamorphosis*. "No," he said. "It's about a salesman," said the therapist "who loses his sense of identity and no longer sees himself as a human being but as a cockroach who lives off of what others leave. In essence, to mask is to fear living up to your potential for growth. It is, in fact, much like assuming someone else's identity because yours is not good enough."

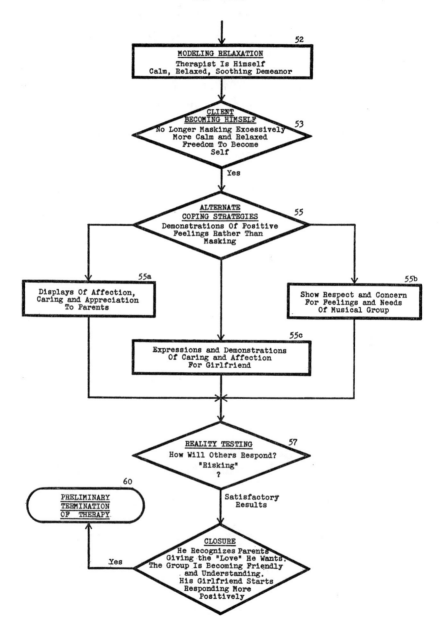

Segment Of

TYPE II PROBLEM INTERVENTION

With "Denny"

MODELING RELAXATION 52
Therapist Is Himself
Calm, Relaxed, Soothing Demeanor

**CLIENT
BECOMING HIMSELF** 53
No Longer Masking Excessively
More Calm and Relaxed
Freedom To Become
Self

Yes

**ALTERNATE
COPING STRATEGIES** 55
Demonstrations Of Positive
Feelings Rather Than
Masking

55a
Displays Of Affection,
Caring and Appreciation
To Parents

55b
Show Respect and Concern
For Feelings and Needs
Of Musical Group

55c
Expressions and Demonstrations
Of Caring and Affection
For Girlfriend

REALITY TESTING 57
How Will Others Respond?
"Risking"
?

Satisfactory
Results

60
**PRELIMINARY
TERMINATION
OF THERAPY**

CLOSURE
He Recognizes Parents
Giving the "Love" He Wants.
The Group Is Becoming Friendly
and Understanding.
His Girlfriend Starts
Responding More
Positively

Yes

Figure 13

"Yeah," he said, "I can see that—and seeing it makes all the difference in the world."

Denny and his therapist have not seen each other for a while now. His profession keeps him on the move. Like most musicians, he spends very little time at home but does write and occasionally calls to let his therapist know how things are going. At this point, the prognosis looks good.

MOVING TOWARD PEOPLE

Although Mat and Denny posed some interesting challenges, the person who really needed help was Paul. When he first applied for therapy, he had done so as the result of a seminar he had attended on nexus psychotherapy. He was a participant in the seminar and was, as a matter of fact, one of the most active therapists in the question-and-answer session immediately following the presentation.

THE CASE OF PAUL

Paul was young, perhaps twenty-seven, tall, handsome, friendly, and quite distinguished looking. His colleagues seemed to respond well to his presence and appeared to gravitate toward him whenever he was available. His most impressive quality was, perhaps, the way he dressed. Although all of his colleagues were well dressed, Paul always seemed to have an edge on them. He dressed like a professional, and the extent of his attire always seemed just a bit more sophisticated than did that of his colleagues. As a therapist, he practiced both on the university campus and in the privacy of his own home. He had been quite successful in his practice and had recently closed in a section of his house, converting it into a large office and group therapy area.

HIS DESPERATION. His request for professional services came late one evening after the seminar on nexus therapy had long ended. The therapist had returned to his hotel room, spent some time working on his seminar papers, and was just about to retire when the phone rang. Paul was on the other end and asked if he could come over. The therapist said, "Fine, come on over," and in fifteen minutes, Paul was there. He said that, after listening to the seminar that night, he thought he would like to discuss some of his feelings. From the very inception of the relationship, he made it quite clear that he had been under therapeutic care for a number of years and had recently become rather desperate because he could find no one with whom he could discuss his own problems. Not only was his therapist in another section of the country, but he had some reservations about how well his past therapy had gone. He started by talking about his past, his parents, his friends, and his family. During the next few hours, he left an impression which became increasingly more vivid. The more he talked, the more immature he seemed. Much of what he said left the impression that he constantly sought attention, that he behaved seductively in an effort to get people to do what he wanted, that he never really searched within himself for personal identity but always hoped to find it through imitation. His life seemed to consist of masking, assuming roles, and imitating others. Because masking was so easy, he sometimes visualized himself as an actor on the stage of life—playing to an audience of colleagues, patients, and observers. In a way, it gave him the opportunity to take on the identity of the characters he played. Obviously, one of those roles was as the well-groomed psychotherapist.

When he first entered the room, the therapist said, "How are you?" to which Paul responded,

Since you asked, and you'll be sorry you did, Paul is alive and depressed and slowly dying a little more each day.

I pray you are well — (pause)

I gotta be dying! Things have become hopelessly f . . . . up. I'm convinced that I'm getting around to paying my "final dues." I wish you could understand how f . . . . up I am.

His Dramatic Bent. Traditionally, Paul had a flair for the dramatic. Even now there was a touch of drama about him. Desperate as his words seemed, he reflected a sense of personal warmth, lightheartedness, and flexibility. Yet, there was a kind of mechanical, depersonalized shallowness in his tone. The therapist, as his listener, recognized that he was seemingly talking at one emotional level and feeling at another. The incongruency of what he was saying as opposed to what he was feeling seemed much like the conflicting pattern of a hebephrenic. At times, it seemed like he was "putting the therapist on," *i.e.* attempting to make his conflict serious enough so that he could seduce the therapist. As the therapist continued to listen, however, Paul suddenly shifted gears.

I came down here some time ago and went to work as a therapist. No trouble with that. I worked at the university for a while and then started a private practice. Before coming here, I was under psychiatric treatment. My psychiatrist was George B . . . . You probably know of him. He was a colleague of mine. Not really a friend. We worked on the staff at F . . . . , but I left to come here. Yeah, here — my big break! Finally landed a university position. Jesus! What a Chinese fire drill.

Almost as bad as the place I left. In the midst of my search for self-discovery, I discovered that the administrators were ripping off the university. When I raised my squeaky voice, I was bombed — you know? Fired! Zapped!

To celebrate this sterling occasion, my wife divorced me two days later, took the children to her ancestral burial grounds, and now spends her time preparing letters to me telling me they're still alive — whatever that means. I even heard from my kids — once — I think? I'm ready to throw in the towel!

HIS SEARCH FOR IDENTITY. As Paul said this, he apparently felt depressed. In this respect, his feelings were much like Mat's and Denny's. But unlike Mat and Denny, he used a different method of movement. Mat withdrew from his relationships with people. Denny moved against people, and Paul moved toward people. Interestingly enough, all three experienced depression. Why? Because the coping strategies they were using were not working. In each case, the strategies were learned methods of responding which were simply neither bringing the security, satisfaction, or pleasure nor avoiding the pain, fear, or dissatisfaction each had anticipated. The failure of each person's method was directly related to the person's inability to see himself as a subjective part of his relationships rather than as an objective bystander.

Because Paul was not always sure of what role he should play, he sometimes shifted topics simply to avoid any type of confrontation. When he said, "When I raised my squeaky voice, I was bombed—you know? Fired! Zapped!" he wanted his therapist to know that he was not really protesting to the administrators but simply commenting. The threat he posed to the administrators was too great, however, and he was fired. But it should be noted that he did not withdraw nor did he attack.

HIS PARENTS. During the weeks that his therapist saw him, it appeared that his feelings of insecurity resulted more from his relationship with his parents than from anything else. At first, it was difficult to determine just what that relationship was like. Eventually, the relationship led to the point where he discovered that, although he loved his parents a great deal, he had one experience during his childhood which was truly traumatic for him. When he was quite young—as best he could remember, about seven—his parents maintained a foster home for children. He found great delight in playing with the children who stayed at his home and was pleased to have them as playmates. What he had forgotten was that, during this same period, his playmates suddenly left. Sometimes there were long periods of time when he was alone. It was during one of these periods when he was by himself that he discovered a check on the dressing table. Because there were no other children in the house, and because the departure of each foster child was followed by a check similar to this one, he assumed that his parents were about to sell him. At that particular moment, he lost his sense of identity. Since he loved his parents, it was difficult for him to respond aggressively. His only recourse seemed to be to assume a different role. Perhaps it was at this point that he thought more seriously about how to control his environment. Naturally, one way of doing this was to become super good—so good that when he did something wrong, his parents frequently wondered why they were so bad.

Over a period of years, Paul gradually became a debonair therapist, a smooth talking professional who, on the outside, seemed to be a warm and friendly person, while on the inside, he was a seething mass of depersonalization and repression. His method for maintaining a semblance of balance was to be as flexible as possible. To Paul, this meant never taking a stand on an issue. When he had no direction, he simply followed someone who seemed to have direction. If anyone questioned him about an issue he was attempting to avoid, he would immediately identify his position by referring to or quoting some authority.

Some years ago, Bandura and Walters (1967) did an interesting article in which they talked about social learning and dependent behavior. In it, they referred to Carins' research (1962) and how parents who encouraged and reward dependency also serve as nurturant models for their children. It seems, from what Paul told me, that he was very close to his parents—that he did, in fact, love his parents very much. Apparently, his relationship was such that there was much positive reinforcement for him within the family, and this intensified his dependency. When he first saw the check and then gradually arrived at an interpretation of what it meant, it was this dependency factor that was threatened. As a child, he was unprepared to cope with his loss of family identity. Without his parents, he could not understand who he was. The anxiety of the experience was so overwhelming that, from that point on, he was unable to trust himself in close relationships with anyone. Unfortunately, his response was based on his misinterpretation of what really happened. Because he perceived the incident incorrectly, the shock of the experience brought about a change in him which caused a different pattern of relating. The consequence of that pattern later led to divorce, depersonalized relations with faculty members, a flare for the dramatic, an inability to find personal identity, and a tendency to overidentify with others. Paul's "Dramatic Syndrome" Learning Route is illustrated in Figure 14.

HIS INSIGHTS. At first, he was terribly shaken by the reality of his repression. Over a period of weeks, he became more composed and once again assumed his flair for the dramatic. After contemplating what he was gradually beginning to learn about himself, he finally said one evening after his final therapy session,

I tell you that I stand here before this awareness of myself looking out over the total horizons of my sheer and utter ignorance — and

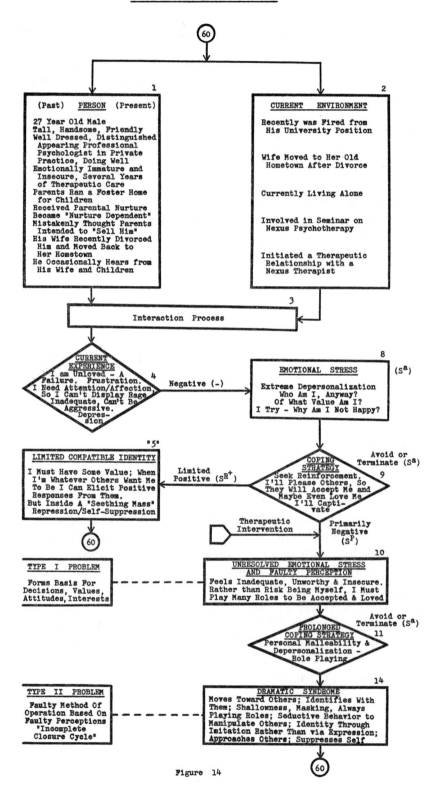

Figure 14

if, as a learned friend of mine (his therapist) put it, this is the first step toward wisdom, then surely, I'm about to become the most brilliant son-of-a-bitch in the world!

Paul left early the next morning. When his therapist next saw him at the last seminar, Paul gave him a note which said,

Yes, I see more clearly now — the love, the hope, the beauty still — if only in my dreams. If the time should come when I'm super down again, I'll remember you and say,

> How am I to thee?
>   this man,
> Who cares to know what I'm about
>   my everywhere.
>
> That I might share
>   this gift from him
> Myself
>
> Come! Join me now
>   show me your Christ
> For I am here to stay.

Paul has long since returned to the midwest to continue his practice. It seems that he will always remain a person who is somewhat different. What he feels intrinsically about the outcome of his therapy is not easily discernible. He writes occasionally and telephones infrequently. Although he never complains, it must be said in all honesty that he is somewhat beyond our comprehension. Whether or not that makes him a totally functioning person is something we may never be sure about. The conclusion must obviously be yours.

RESEARCH

What a therapist does in his practice in terms of his effectiveness and/or accountability is always suspect unless he provides research evidence which indicates that he not only has a consistent system of performing but one which also lends itself well to teaching.

Perhaps, of these problems, the most challenging has been that of measuring therapeutic effectiveness. The complexities of the problem stem from the fact that therapy is not only difficult to define, but is carried out through a process which involves a number of variables which have been difficult to control. Of major concern has been (a) the philosophical basis from which theory emerges, (b) the development or selection of tests by which attitudinal change is measured, and (c) the research design by which behavior change is recorded. The following chapter will reflect on these challenges with specific regard for the concepts introduced throughout this book and with special attention to the concern theorists have shared for so many years relative to the effectiveness of psychotherapy.

CHAPTER 7

EXPLORING THE EFFECTIVENESS OF NEXUS PSYCHOTHERAPY THROUGH RESEARCH

THE DIFFICULTY INVOLVED in researching effectiveness has long existed as one of the most impalpable issues in the profession of psychotherapy. Seemingly, it has caused a mystique about the profession which is difficult to disestablish. Perhaps this problem emerges as much from the lack of an operational definition of psychotherapy as it does from the problem of converting such a definition into some form of pragmatic action. It is not difficult to realize that, without some form of objectivity by which psychotherapy can be reduced to a science of human understanding, the method by which its effectiveness can be measured fails to exist. Thus, psychotherapy, at best, must rely upon a definition, the results of which become discernible only through practice.

In an effort to test the validity of this thesis, the authors combined forces with Royce Kenston Mueller* to do a rather comprehensive survey of research literature devoted to the effectiveness of psychotherapy. As a result of this survey, it was concluded that psychotherapy is both an art and a science. Recognizing it as such seemed appropriate because the literature indicates that it deals with the art of forming relationships and the science of understanding such relationships. In practice, however, it is probably best recognized as one of several social sciences of communicating. Seemingly, its primary purpose in practice is to blend the subjectivity of human understanding with the objectivity of

---

*Dr. Mueller is currently serving as a staff psychologist with the Alaska Psychiatric Institute, Anchorage, Alaska.

human examination. This is particularly true of nexus psychotherapy. As a matter of fact, one might even say that nexus therapy is a science, based on the theoretical premise that learning to relate serves as an antecedent to complete fulfillment; and an art, based on the idea that if man is to be mentally healthy, he must live in the present rather than in the past. It might also be said that nexus therapy is the means by which man is encouraged to go out from himself and to search for identity rather than to withdraw from life and permit his identity to be imposed on him. Basically, it is the means by which man learns to risk himself within the confines of the world in which he lives. Ultimately, it is the means by which he finds identity within that world and fulfillment within himself.

SOME SPECULATIONS ABOUT RELATING AND RESEARCH

As a result of our survey, we also conclude that, although psychotherapy is an area which is frequently researched, it is still plagued by the discontent of vagueness; there are still questions about the benefits of psychotherapy. Thus, it became apparent that any attempt to research nexus psychotherapy would have to concern itself with three basic problems: the selection and utilization of instruments designed to measure change, the statistical implications for measuring change, and the philosophical basis from which a research design most naturally seemed to emerge. What we did was this:

A. Because we recognized that we had to establish criteria against which we could measure change, we used three basic instruments: (1) the Psychological Screening Inventory (PSI), which is a standardized instrument; (2) the Corsini Q-Sort, which is also standardized; and (3) the Emotional Stress Checklist (ESC), which we designed as a means of tabulating the extent of emotional stress in terms of the number the stress characteristics shown by the client.

B. Because we recognized that previous research methods in this area were designed to be used primarily with groups rather than with individuals, we explored the possibility of a new own-control type of research. It was obvious that, although some extremely sophisticated research designs had been worked out through the use of prewait and postwait designs, evidence that movement had taken place was always suspect because the inner controls and the intricate samplings of subgroups essential for such designs had remained rather questionable. Then, too, it appeared to us that past researchers had approached what seemed to be an idiographic problem through the use of a nomothetic approach. In essence, we felt that the parametric statistics designed exclusively for group-to-group comparisons obviously ignored the relationship a person has with himself at any two given time intervals in his life, the "person-to-himself" variability that appears as a consequence of the time factor alone.

C. We recognized man as an idiosyncratic entity. What that meant to us was that only he could define for us where he was in his search for a better life. That is, we did not intend to intrude our values into the life of another, but rather to get him to define for us where he wanted to go and how he wanted to get there. We recognized the fact that such an approach could be criticized because it is the consensus of some researchers that emotionally stressed people have a reduced potential to think realistically. Our experience dictated the belief that anyone who could think realistically, reduced potential or not, was capable of establishing personal goals and determining what his progress toward these goals had been. From an existential point of view then, we said that, if a person who was in the process of becoming had some impression of what he wanted to become and where he was relative to that objective, then he was serving as his own-control. To establish a basis from which self-actualizing changes could be measured, we used the Corsini Q-Sort. We felt from previous experiences with this instrument that, when Ideal Self sorts were consistently high over a long period of time, they defined a person's self-actualizing goals in life, while Real Self sorts defined where the person was relative to these goals. Then, too, it seemed logical to believe that the consistency with which a person maintained a concept of an Ideal Self would attest to his ability to think realistically, while his relative position in terms of that Ideal Self would attest to his personal growth. We felt that the approach had merit simply because sort techniques are designed to mask the impact of direct comparisons and, thus, make it impossible for a person doing sorts to determine how one sort compared with another.

Thus, it became obvious that one approach to working within the realm of these three factors was to include an own-control research design in which each person was asked to establish a concept of self-actualization and then to establish where he was relative to that concept. Such an own-control design would, it seemed, circumvent many of the difficulties heretofore found in research of this nature simply because of its potential existential implications. Unlike the traditional own-control designs with groups, however, the single own-control design required that the definition of change be in the hands of the person experiencing such change and not in the hands of the experimenter. This lack of intrusion into the person's life established a precedent for the utilization of an existential approach to a research design which, up to this point in time, had not yet been attempted.

Since it seemed reasonable to believe that a person who was capable of reality thinking could establish a constant Ideal Self Concept, it also seemed reasonable to believe that this same person could reflect the extent to which his Real Self Concept approached such an Ideal Self Concept. Logic, itself, seemed to dictate the idea that any person who was capable of reality thinking and had proven his ability to remain consistent in the formation of self-actualizing goals would also be capable of reflecting his progress toward such goals. To ask a man to establish his own concept of self-actualization and then to record his movements toward such a concept is a real challenge in research, for it demands that the approach be subtle enough to measure change without any indication of how that measurement is taking place. That is, the task of setting an objective and measuring movement must be put to the person in the form of something other than a popularity contest, *i.e.* a questionnaire, a checklist, or a rating scale which in some way has been designed to view his opinion of how much he has been helped. Therefore, we felt that whatever we used not only had to measure attitudinal changes but also had to assess individual movement. While past statistics dealt primarily with group movement, our design dealt both with group and individual movement.

TESTING NEW IDEAS THROUGH RESEARCH

To implement our design, we trained six counseling psychologists to relate on the basis of the constructs normally taught in nexus psychotherapy during the second phase of our training program at the University of Southern Mississippi. The training took nine weeks and was actually a complementary experience since all of the therapists involved in the project had previously been employed in professional helping relations.

The subjects used were divided into three groups consisting of (1) self-referrals (E_1), (2) subjects referred by others (E_2), and controls (C). All three groups were matched in size (N = 10; Total = 30), age, need for therapeutic services, and their ability to Q-Sort an Ideal Self Concept with consistency. Each subject in the E_1 and E_2 groups received one hour of individual therapy two times per week for approximately nine weeks. The subjects in the control group received no comparable service.

To make certain that the emotional stress experienced by all subjects was comparable, the Psychological Screening Inventory (PSI) was employed as a basic screening technique. Previous research by Craig G. Schoon and Robert F. Stahmann (1971) indicated that this instrument was capable of identifying profiles which reflected emotional stress.

On the basis of what Schoon and Stahmann (1971) found, three judges were asked to sort the PSI profiles into two categories: (a) an apparent need for therapeutic services and (b) no apparent need for therapeutic services. The interrater reliability indices between judges ranged from .80 to .92 *(see* Table IV) .

Since we felt that the PSI was capable of yielding profile data

TABLE IV

SCREENING OF SUBJECTS FROM PSI PROFILES
INTERRATER RELIABILITY INDICES

Judges	Experimental Group	Control Group
A & B	.90	.83
A & C	.90	.92
B & C	.80	.84

which made it possible to discern emotionally stressed subjects, we also used it after the completion of therapy to discern movement away from emotional stress.

For data pertaining to self-actualizing tendencies, we used the Corsini Q-Sort (1956). This particular Q-Sort consists of fifty adjectives which are sorted according to a normal distribution (Stephenson, 1953). The adjectives are printed on cards which are sorted into ten columns, five adjectives in each column. Those adjectives on the extreme left are least like the rated object; those on the extreme right, most like the object. In this particular case, each participant was asked to sort both a Real Self Concept and an Ideal Self Concept. Any Real Self movement toward the Ideal Self Concept was then used to define self-actualizing tendencies. This meant that, if a person had a Real Self Concept which moved toward his Ideal Self Concept while his Ideal Self Concept remained relatively constant over any given period of time, it could be assumed that the person was in the process of self-actualizing.

The third instrument we used for assessment of movement was the Emotional Stress Checklist (ESC). We structured the ESC on the basis of characteristics used to define specific emotional stress syndromes and employed it as a means of testing our concept of effectiveness (Gutsch and Peters, 1973). The way we hoped to demonstrate effectiveness was by taping initial and final therapy sessions, taking thirty-minute samples from these hour-long tapes, and doing a strict classification of all emotional stress characteristics reflected by clients during these therapy sessions.

Initially, what we did was to use the Alienation and Discomfort Scales from the PSI to screen emotionally stressed subjects. We did this to determine what change, if any, took place as a result of therapy and whether or not such change, if it did occur, was toward self-actualization. The ESC was used to verify the fact that such behavior change took place and that the movement complemented the results from both the PSI and the Q-Sort techniques.

In an effort to establish a concept of self-actualization, each potential subject was asked to sort his Ideal Self Concept. The key to selection was his ability to make these sorts at two specific time intervals and to do so with consistency. As a "cut-off" for consistency, we used a Pearson product moment correlation of .70. We felt that the correlation was sufficiently high since the instrument guidelines suggest a .60 baseline correlation between a Real Self Sort and Sort By Others for any two people who plan to be married. Each subject was asked to do two Real Self Sorts, i.e. one immediately preceding the first therapy session and one immediately preceding the final therapy session. These two sorts were compared with the Ideal Self Sort which, because of its consistency, served as a constant. By doing this, it was possible to assess the effectiveness of nexus therapy in terms of the movement of the Real Self toward the Ideal Self at the inception of therapy and again at the end of those services. Once Real Self movement was recorded for these two periods of time, the movement toward the Ideal Self Concept could be measured and compared with PSI changes and ESC changes.

THE ESC: INTERRATER RELIABILITY AND INTRARATER STABILITY

Of these three instruments, the one which was considered suspect was the Emotional Stress Checklist, primarily because it was constructed by the experimenters. To remove some of the doubts researchers might normally have about such an instrument, we subjected it to a number of tests of reliability. First, we wondered whether or not people who were employed in professional helping relations such as psychotherapy could score taped interviews with consistency if we gave them nothing more than a checklist of syndrome characteristics with a brief explanation of how these characteristics were to be recognized and scored. Second, we wondered whether or not the three raters who scored tapes would produce high interscorer and intrascorer reliability coefficients.

Specifically, what we did to investigate interrater agreement and intrarater stability was to take a 25 percent sample of those taped sessions that could be rated. Ultimately, what happened was that twenty of the forty tapes initially made had been precluded from the study for two reasons: first, many of the tapes were of poor audio quality and literally impossible to rate; second, some tapes contained comments by monitoring supervisors which contaminated the audio sections.

To determine interrater reliability, five randomly selected tapes were rated twice by each of three raters, providing interrater reliability coefficients ranging from a low of .63 to a high of .83 using the Bijou technique (Table V). Using SAX's popular

TABLE V

BIJOU INTERRATER RELIABILITY COEFFICIENTS

All Raters At Two Times	Tapes Selected				
	3	4	7	10	17
T_1	.63	.67	.70	.83	.69
T_2	.82	.83	.64	.68	.70

percentage approach, we found a low of .63 and a high of .96 (Table VI). Essentially, the indices of interrater reliability were obtained through the use of three procedures: (1) a procedure described by Bijou (1968), (2) a popular percentage approach mentioned by Sax (1968), and (3) a test of significance between mean ratings at two times to provide an indication of rater consistency over time (Tables V and VII).

Intrarater stability was obtained by asking each rater to rerate his tapes after a period of from one to three weeks. Results indicated coefficients ranging from .56 to .99 (Table VIII).

Note that the third procedure involved pooling the ratings for each tape and completing a test to examine the statistical signifi-

TABLE VI

COEFFICIENTS OF INTERRATER AGREEMENT
in PERCENT

Raters Contrasted	Tapes Selected				
	3 T_1 T_2	4 T_1 T_2	7 T_1 T_2	10 T_1 T_2	17 T_1 T_2
A vs. B	.63 .92	.85 .83	.76 .77	.87 .88	.80 .70
A vs. C	.94 .90	.67 .90	.93 .64	.96 .68	.85 .96
B vs. C	.67 .82	.79 .92	.71 .84	.83 .78	.69 .72

TABLE VII

CONSISTENCY OF RATINGS OVER TIME DURATION FROM
ONE TO THREE WEEKS

	Mean Ratings		
Tapes	T_1	T_2	t*
3	87.333	98.00	1.228
4	83.00	83.666	.054
7	77.333	109.333	2.196
10	96.333	83.667	1.433
17	91.333	93.000	.281

*t (.05) = 2.776

TABLE VIII

COEFFICIENTS OF INTRARATER STABILITY PERCENT

	Tapes Selected				
Rater	3	4	7	10	17
A	.95	.74	.96	.95	.88
B	.72	.95	.56	.80	.99
C	.89	.82	.67	.75	.94

cance between the mean ratings at T_1 and T_2. This was done to test for the stability of these ratings over time, *i.e.* the probability that the same ratings over time, due to the rating procedure, is beyond chance occurrence (Table VII). The lowest scores were, in all cases, the first attempts of scorers to rate their own tapes or those of others.

Interestingly enough, the high interrater and intrarater reliability coefficients gave us the *sine qua non* which we felt we needed to establish an operational definition of effectiveness

EMOTIONAL STRESS CHARACTERISTICS: TRAINING FOR RECOGNITION

The method we used in training raters to recognize emotional stress characteristics involved having them study a statement made by Mat. Raters were told to examine the following statement taken from the case of Mat.

> I'm so afraid of failure that I don't even try a second time.[1] (pause) You know what I mean? I don't try because I'm afraid to fail.[2] (pause) I don't believe in the old proverb — "Try, Try again" — Once I fail, That's it.[3] (pause) Even though I may try again, I think, "Well, why try? You'll just fail."[4] I don't have any self-confidence.[5] I have to be tricked into doing things.[6] Then, when something goes right, I say, "Did I really do that or was it just luck!"[7] I can't even develop self-confidence.[8]

They were advised to look at how the individual statements were numbered and told that the technique was related to syndromes originally introduced by Gutsch and Peters (1973).

The personal training of raters included an orientation to each syndrome, i.e. an understanding of how clusters of words or phrases are frequently used by people attempting to cope with unique life experiences. They also learned that such characteristics were accompanied by stressful situations—situations experienced as a client attempts to cope with the infinite struggle of moving beyond his present situation; as he attempts to grow or develop or transcend what he is and where he is.

In completing this exercise, we asked raters to study the transcribed statement of Mat and then to rate each numbered response with an awareness of both content and feeling. To do this, the raters were asked to place a tally mark on the Emotional Stress Checklist (Fig. 15) to the left of the characteristic they felt best described the emotional response being indicated by each emo-

EMOTIONAL STRESS CHECKLIST

Dispirited

		Rigid	
Loss of interest	Feelings of remorse	Precise	Self-doubting
Unable to concentrate	Feels rejected	Meticulous	Indecisive
Low spirits	Low self-concept	Methodical	Inadequate
Feels let-down	Experiences insomnia	Exacting	Lacks affection
Feelings of despair	Loss of appetite	Over-conscientious	Guilt-laden
Feels depressed	Excessive sleeping	Irreversible	Submissive
Hopelessness	Marked nervousness	Unyielding	Defensive
Futility about life	Lack of energy	Perfectionistic	Projects blame
Gradual withdrawal	Somatic complaints	Driven	Insensitive to others
Talks of suicide	Excessive fatigue	Obsessive	Hypercritical
Self-accusatory	Frequent colds	Worries over trifles	Evaluative
		Preoccupied with details	Judgmental

Impulsive

	Dramatic	
Acts in haste	Immature	Shallow relationships
Feels restless	Behaves seductively	Feels depersonalized
Shows no remorse	Seeks attention	Appears helpless
Shows poor self-control	Assumes roles	Flights of imagination
Has outbursts	Warm	Massive repression
Rejects convention	Flexible	Over-identification
Poorly controlled by others	Lacks identity	Personality compartmentalization
Does antisocial acts	Has others identity	Conversion reaction
Independent	Flair for the dramatic	Limited intellectual drive
	Easily influenced	Lacks studious commitment
	Imitates others	Spirits up — high
	Shifting feelings	

Compulsive

	Anxiety	*Negative inference*
Fears failure	Cue	
Fears rejection by others	Affect	
Expresses fear object	Primary reaction	

Figure 15.

tional   stress or negative statement made by the client. They
were reminded by written instructions that a response could be
judged emotional if it seemed to be part of a broader negative
attitude, belief, perception, or feeling, *i.e.* whether it was related
to the general concept of emotional stress as it is herein defined.
Whether or not the client's reaction to his situation was, in their
opinion, justified was not relevant. What was relevant was that
they recognize the emotional stress characteristics. We instructed
them to remember that people respond in many ways and that it
was our contention that their response patterns were made by
choice and, therefore, told a significant story about what they felt
and what they were like.   It was assumed that, at any given moment, a person has a number of alternative responses from which
he can choose. Yet, the very fact that he makes some rather specific choices indicates that he subscribes to certain beliefs, both
about himself and about the world in which he lives.

INSTRUCTIONS FOR USING THE ESC

Generally speaking, the instructions for recording emotional
stress characteristics were quite simple. Raters were instructed (a)
to listen for negative inferences, (b) how to recognize such inferences, and (c) how to record the emotional stress characteristics.

Briefly, what they did was to examine the numbered responses
and study the composite thoughts which were being conveyed.
Their guidelines gave them the following orientations: (Fig. 15)

(a) The first three numbered responses are recognized as state-
    ments of gradual withdrawal. The first statement indicates
    a fear of failure which ultimately leads to feelings of hope-
    lessness, despair, and futility as indicated in the next two
    statements.

(b) In responses four and five, Mat is reflecting a note of de-
    pression over anticipated failure. In response number
    four, he is showing some indication of optimism. That is,
    it seems that what he is saying is that he would like to try
    again but does not want to fail. In response number five,
    he gives a reason for not trying again.

(c) The sixth response is a very clever statement. It is Mat's cushion, the method by which he can excuse his failures, as he says, "I have no self-confidence." It seems that he is willing to risk but only if he has some excuse to fall back on in the event of failure. Apparently, this is an attempt to protect his self-image, what he feels he should be as a person.

(d) The seventh and eighth responses reflect self-doubt and futility. Interestingly, his self-doubt in response number seven is really self-accusatory. It relates to response number six and gives the impression that Mat is really saying, "I'm not good enough to do anything right, so don't expect it of me." To this extent, it is self-accusatory.

To score Mat's responses, you simply tally the number of emotional stress characteristics made and enter the specific areas of stress on the Emotional Stress Checklist (ESC).

Special instructions governing the scoring covered difficulties originally encountered when the instructions were pilot tested. For the purposes of clarification, the raters were given the following additional information:

(a) As you study the statements in this exercise, ask yourself, "Is the person responding in an emotional way?" If so, "What characteristics is he reflecting which indicate emotional stress?" Whenever you have made a decision, look through the ESC and tally your response on the Checklist and to the left of the characteristic that best describes your client's statement. When you find it difficult to tally a response, simply place it in the section referred to as Negative Inference. After practicing for awhile, you will find that the characteristics can be classified with greater ease. Difficult classifications are sometimes experienced when a person makes a negative statement relating to nonpersonal or potentially neutral topics. For example, when Mat said, "I have to be tricked into doing things," this was scored as an emotional stress characteristic because he was making a negative remark about himself. It was like

saying, "I'm not capable of making decisions because I'm
such a hopeless person."

(b) Each emotional response should be recorded once, even
though the person making the response uses several similar
adjectives within his basic statement. For example, Mat's
comment, "I'm so afraid of failure that I don't even try a
second time," is one basic statement and is given one tally
mark. If he had said, "I'm so afraid—life is so frightening—
I'm so scared, I can't even try again." This would still
have received only one tally mark because the adjectives
used were an extension of a single thought.

(c) When studying responses, it becomes apparent that certain
things are predominant, *i.e.* certain topics seem to be discussed with consistency. When such a sequence occurs,
the emotional stress characteristics are tallied singularly
when there is no perseveration of thought. For example,
when Mat said, "Even though I may try again, I think,
'Well, why try? You'll just fail.' " This is an independent
thought and is tallied as such. The thoughts which precede it and those which follow are all independent of this
statement. Perseveration would have occurred if Mat had
said, "Even though I may try again, I think, 'Well, why try?
You'll just fail.' "—and followed it with, "I'd like to try
again, but I don't want to fail."

Remember as you complete your ratings that the significance
of understanding the syndrome rests with the way you will ultimately respond to the person. That is, the understandings you
have about a person as a result of recognizing his specific patterns
of coping may serve as the basis for helping him to understand
what he must do to initiate a successful pattern of change.

Remember that to understand the syndrome is to understand
how the characteristics which define emotional stress either increase or decrease and, thus, whether or not a person is moving in
the direction of greater stress or improved stability. This understanding not only tells the therapist where he is in his relationship
with the client, but how the client is moving in an effort to bring
about change.

ESC MOVEMENT AND Q-SORT RESULTS

To establish a criterion against which ESC effectiveness could be reaffirmed, specific Q-Sort results were correlated and then plotted graphically. Each of the subjects was asked to Q-sort an Ideal Self-Concept. Since self-referred clients (E_1 subjects) were given service immediately, a Pearson product-movement correlation between the Ideal Self-Concept at the inception of therapy and Ideal Self-Concept at the termination of therapy determined the constancy of the subject's Ideal Self and, therefore, of this concept of a self-actualizing goal.

Subjects referred by others were exposed to a prewait period of five weeks, during which time the constancy of the Ideal Self-Conceptions were checked. This became a criterion for inclusion as a member of the E_2 group. Members of the group were, for the most part, hostile subjects who were referred to therapy and had to comply in order to meet specific recommendations made by university faculty members. Whereas the subjects from the E_1 group were self-referred and requested services immediately, the subjects from the E_2 group were referred by others and expressed some reluctance toward the imposition of such services.

PLOTTING SELF-ACTUALIZING TENDENCIES

To plot the movement of all subjects through the use of Q-Sort results, all participants and potential participants were required to do Real Self and Ideal Self sorts. Because the time element differed for subjects and was designated by virtue of the time they walked in or were referred, we always defined the inception of therapy as time one (T_1) and the termination of therapy as time two (T_2). The span between the T_1 and T_2 periods designated the time period during which each subject in each of the two experimental groups received individual therapy. Movements were then plotted in terms of Real Self to Ideal Self movement. By plotting these individual movements graphically, it was possible to reaffirm operationally, and in terms of observable movement, the precise direction of movement and the exact distance covered by that movement.

To record the Real Self concept plots (RS_1, RS_2) as they moved in terms of the subject's Ideal Self constancy (r:IS_1 ↔ IS_2), relationships of the sorts were plotted on double square root paper according to the following guide (Figs. 16, 17, 18, 19, and 20):

(a) A *horizontal* line was plotted representing the correlation between IS_1 and IS_2, the criterion against which therapeutic effectiveness was reaffirmed. For example, if the IS_1 ↔ IS_2 correlation between T_1 and T_2 was .80, then the IS plot looked like this:

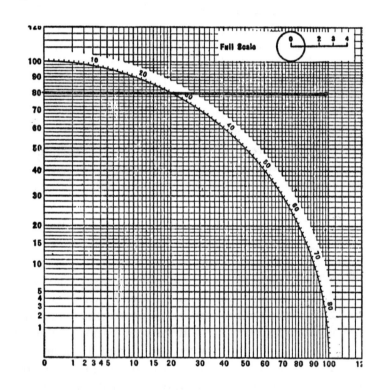

Figure 16

(b) A *vertical* line was plotted representing the correlation between RS₁ and IS₁. Assuming that the RS₁, IS₁ r = .40, the first vertical plot looked like this:

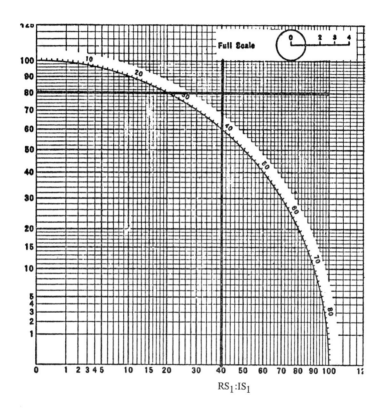

Figure 17

(c) A second *vertical* plot was constructed by correlating RS_2 and IS_2. Assuming that the second correlation was .80, the second plot looked like this:

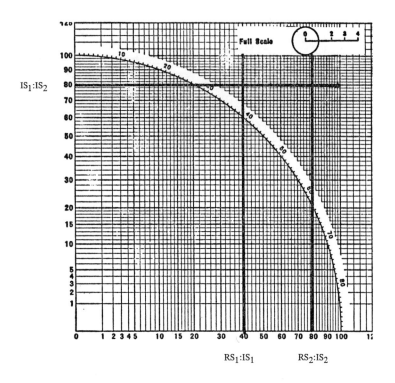

Figure 18

(d) Coordinating lines #1 and #2 were then plotted from point zero on the horizontal-vertical axes to points where the vertical plots $RS_1:IS_1$ and $RS_2:IS_2$ intersect with the horizontal plot $IS_1:IS_2$. The results looked like this:

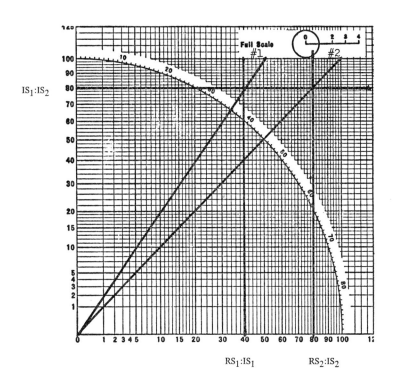

$RS_1:IS_1$ $RS_2:IS_2$

Figure 19

(e) Once this was done, movement could be measured in terms of the broken line plot extended from point "a" of the first intersection coordinate to point "b" of the second intersection coordinate at a 90° angle.

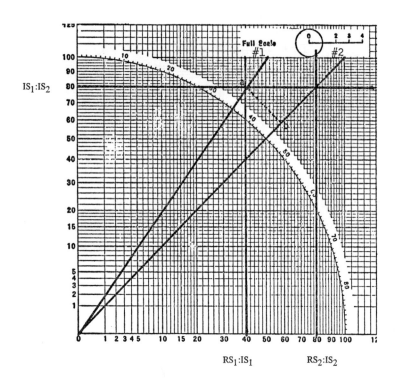

Figure 20

(f) The dotted line also indicates the extent of the movement. The correlation indicates whether or not it was positive and the dotted line represents an approximate standard normal varible (K). The rationale for this technique is explained by W.A. Wallis and H.V. Roberts (1956).

Ultimately, such plots served as a basis for measuring individual movement as well as group movement. Once these plots had been made, the effectiveness of therapy was determined by computing t ratios to determine the significance of differences between (a) mean Z scores, representing the correlations for each group on each PSI factor, and (b) mean emotional stress characteristics, tallied at T_1 and T_2 for each experimental group on the ESC.

RESULTS OF THE STUDY

The establishment of a constant Ideal Self Concept for each of the thirty subjects was the first and foremost consideration in this study. We felt this step essential because we could not consider the subject reliable unless participants demonstrated an ability to maintain IS consistency (r = .70 or above) over a given period of time (Table IX).

TABLE IX

IDEAL SELF CONSTANTS: $IS_1 - IS_2$ PEARSON r'S AND
CORRESPONDING FISHER'S z COEFFICIENTS

E_1 Group (N = 10)		E_2 Group (N = 10)		C Group (N = 10)	
r	z	r	z	r	z
.85	1.26	.89	1.42	.92	1.59
.81	1.13	.71	.89	.75	.97
.80	1.10	.89	1.42	.70	.87
.85	1.26	.81	1.13	.76	1.00
.83	1.19	.74	.95	.85	1.26
.77	1.02	.70	.87	.81	1.13
.85	1.26	.74	.95	.79	1.07
.71	.89	.94	1.74	.82	1.16
.78	1.05	.72	.91	.80	1.10
.82	1.16	.78	1.05	.82	1.16

Once the individual plots were made, a variable K was obtained, in full scale units, for each individual's movement. Figures 21, 22, and 23 show how these plots looked for each of the individuals, while Figure 24 indicates how the movement looked by the groups E_1, E_2, and C (Figs. 21, 22, 23, and 24).

The most obvious interpretation of these data is that those subjects who were self-referred (E_1 group members) moved significantly, while those subjects who were referred by others (E_2 members) and control subjects show comparatively small movements.

CONTROL GROUP ANALYSIS

One of the truly interesting results was that, although the control group seemed to have some positive movement toward self-actualization, there was no corollary movement on the PSI to substantiate this movement. Looking forward to the idiographic analysis as presented in Table XVI, it becomes apparent that the control group experienced considerable variability and that, although six subjects reflected gradual gains, three reflected dramatic gains. Rechecking with these three subjects to determine what transpired during this period, we found that each of the three had experienced rather unique relationship problems. One subject, a young woman, had been deeply depressed when taking the Q-Sort for the first time. During the interim period included by our research, she had managed to form a better relationship with her husband. Apparently, this made her feel somewhat better about herself yet made no real difference in her PSI profile. Thus, the initial course of her marital problems may be without resolution; we strongly suspect that she will continue to have conflicts because the initial change reflected by Q-Sort results has not become manifest in her relations with others, *i.e.* her PSI profile did not change.

The two remaining control subjects who made dramatic gains felt that, within their respective family constellations, they had experienced greater latitude than they had ever before had. They felt they were becoming more responsible and mature in their actions. Although this seemed to make them feel better about them-

Figure 21

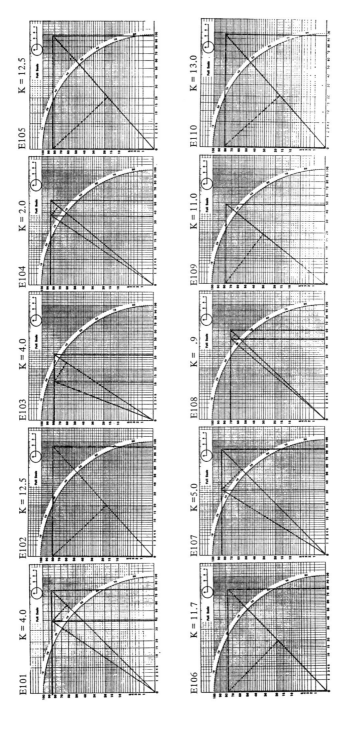

DIRECTION AND EXTENT OF RS - IS MOVEMENT FOR
E₁ SUBJECTS A D INDICATED BY VARIABLE K

Figure 22

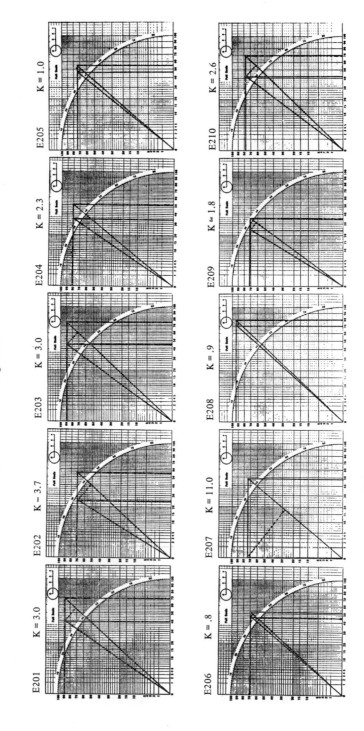

DIRECTION AND EXTENT OF RS - IS MOVEMENT FOR
E_2 SUBJECTS AS INDICATED BY VARIABLE K

Figure 23

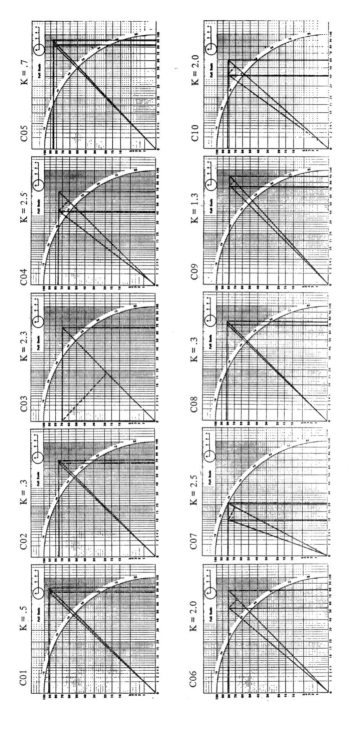

DIRECTION AND EXTENT OF RS - IS MOVEMENT
CONTROL SUBJECTS AS INDICATED BY VARIABLE K

Figure 24

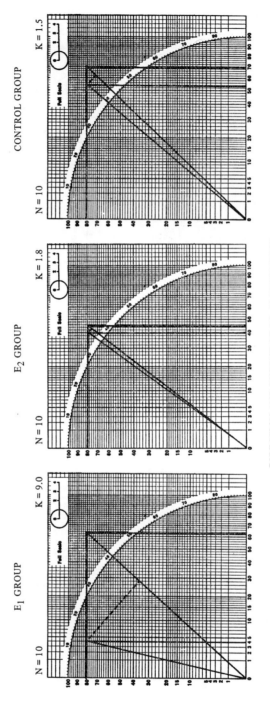

DIRECTION AND EXTENT OF RS - IS MOVEMENT
FOR ALL SUBJECTS (N = 30) AS INDICATED BY VARIABLE K

selves, PSI results indicated that the basic inner problems causing the distortion in their relations with others were not changed. Thus, we expect that they may once again experience similar difficulties at a later date.

The absence of extensive E_2 group movement may well be attributed to the personal reluctance of some of the E_2 subjects to participate in this study. That is, it took so long for us to break through the hostility that prevailed within the therapeutic relationships that the nine weeks we had set aside for the study slipped by before we could reach two of the subjects. Unfortunately, their resistance to therapy was so aggressively exhibited that, upon evaluation, we found negative movements. Obviously, such feelings could indicate that whatever the therapist was doing in the relationship was not appropriate. Checking the tapes quite carefully, we noticed that one particular therapist worked with both of these subjects. Assuming that the negative effect had something to do with how he related to these subjects, we checked his tapes and found that the therapist had attempted to work with symptoms only and not with perception; we felt that he had attempted to modify their behavior by scaling hierarchies of appropriate learning sequences and introducing situations which he felt were most appropriate. Unfortunately, we did not anticipate that one of our therapists would work outside the construct we had originally established for this research. However, after listening to his approach and in all fairness to behaviorists, we must now conclude that he would probably do no better in behavioral therapy than he did with us.

Had it not been for this one erratic episode, the E_2 group might also have proved to move quite well on both the Q-sort and PSI profiles. Such positive results could have encouraged further research on projects designed to look at what impact, if any, therapy might have on emotionally stressed people who have exhibited high degrees of resistance to therapy. In essence, it may well have challenged the belief that only those who are self-referred can be helped.

Results for the E_1 group indicated significantly positive movement on all three instruments; the Q-sort, the ESC, and the PSI.

The Q-sort movement was significant at or beyond the .001 level of confidence; the ESC movement was significant at or beyond the .001 level of confidence; and the PSI movement was significant at or beyond the .01 level of confidence (Tables X, XI, and XII).

TABLE X

PRESENTATION OF z SCORE MEANS, STANDARD DEVIATIONS, AND t RATIOS FOR SELF-REFERRED (E_1) CLIENTS ON THE CORSINI Q-SORT

T_1		T_2		
$\bar{X}$	S.D.	$\bar{X}$	S.D.	t
.041	.3327	.737	.2991	5.494*

*p < .001

TABLE XI

CHECKLIST (ESC) RATINGS FOR SELF-REFERRED (E_1) AND OTHER-REFERRED (E_2) GROUPS: MEANS, STANDARD DEVIATIONS, AND t RATIOS

Group	$\bar{X}_{T_1}$	S.D.	$\bar{X}_{T_2}$	S.D.	t
E_1	125.100	52.717	57.000	31.273	6.100*
E_2	84.400	25.804	76.300	26.249	.739

*p < .001

TABLE XII

PSI MEANS, STANDARD DEVIATIONS, AND t RATIOS FOR SELF-REFERRED (E_1) CLIENTS FOR T_1 AND T_2

Factor	Inception of Counseling (T_1)		Termination of Counseling (T_2)		t
	$\bar{X}$	S.D.	$\bar{X}$	S.D.	
Al	9.500	4.031	6.500	3.324	3.354*
Sn	9.400	4.695	8.600	3.583	1.309
Di	16.000	4.919	7.600	4.758	4.233*
Ex	12.900	4.182	14.500	4.588	1.051
De	9.300	2.147	11.600	2.577	4.116*

p < .01

What these results seem to indicate is that (a) subjects in the E_1 group experienced movement, (b) the movement they experienced was positive, (c) the movement was not an artifact of testing, and (d) positive and effective movement in therapy can be defined and measured.

The precise individual PSI profile changes and how they compared when viewing subjects from the E_1, E_2, and Control groups can be seen by studying Figures 25, 26 and 27 and Tables XIII, XIV, and XV.

CONCLUSIONS

Conclusions that might logically be drawn from this study seem to be that:

(a) Relationships which bring about effective change are possible through appropriate training techniques;

(b) the relatively stable concept of self-actualization as it is defined by each person can serve as a stable criterion factor against which his real self-movement can be measured;

(c) people who experience emotional stress characteristics and are either self-referred or referred by others are capable of defining their own self-actualizing concepts and maintaining these concepts over a period of time with reasonable consistency;

(d) graphing techniques can be useful in own-control research and do, in fact, serve as a basis for plotting movements which can be treated in terms of a standard normal variable K;

(e) the confounding of data which results from pooling measures of personal movement indicates that the value of therapy and, hence, its effectiveness might best be reflected in terms of idiographic data;

(f) the concept of a single control might best be developed further from an existential point of view since the problems introduced by pooling idiographic data do not appear to justify the use of control groups to isolate therapy as the variable which produced the change.

Figure 25

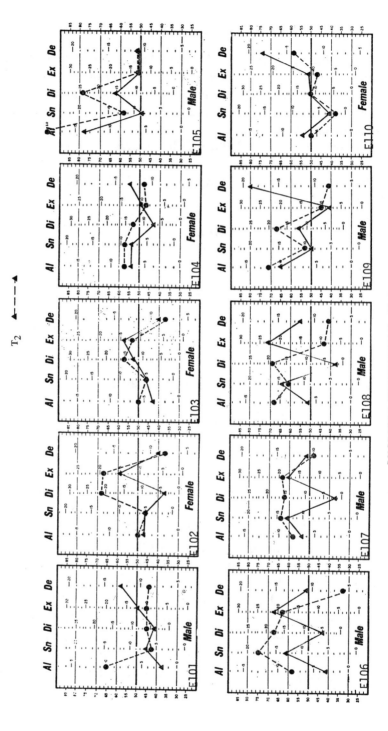

PSI PROFILE CHANGES FOR E₁ SUBJECTS

Credit Richard Lanyon, Author PSI (See Gutsch's corrections)

TABLE XIII

SUMMARY OF MOVEMENT
INDICATIONS FOR SELF-REFERRED (E_1) SUBJECTS

Subjects	Q-Sort RS - IS Relationship				PSI Factors										Emotional Stress Checklist	
					Al		Sn		Di		Ex		De			
	ISC	T_1	T_2	K^*	T_1	T_2	T_1	T_2	T_1	T_2	T_1	T_2	T_1	T_2	T_1	T_2
E101	.85	.39	.80	4,0	10	2	6	7	6	4	10	12	9	13	85	19
E102	.81	-.25	.67	12.5	6	5	5	5	21	4	19	15	8	9	162	62
E103	.80	.13	.33	4.0	6	4	5	5	15	13	12	14	8	9	98	41
E104	.85	.36	.54	2.0	8	7	9	8	13	7	9	10	11	13	62	54
E105	.83	-.25	.74	12.5	20	14	12	9	24	16	13	13	11	11	180	82
E106	.77	-.34	.46	11.7	8	3	18	13	18	5	19	21	6	11	224	118
E107	.85	.32	.85	5.0	8	7	14	13	15	2	19	18	10	11	143	32
E108	.71	.49	.61	.9	11	6	13	14	19	2	9	23	8	12	82	56
E109	.78	-.20	.28	11.0	12	10	10	9	18	12	10	8	8	19	60	14
E110	.82	-.30	.67	13.0	6	7	2	3	11	11	9	11	14	18	155	92

*Full Scale Units on double square root graph paper

DISCUSSION

Perhaps the most obvious interpretation from this data is that the "walk-ins" (E_1 group) moved significantly, the other referred subjects (E_2 group) experienced little or no movement, and the control (C) group experienced some contingencies which by chance influenced the way they felt about themselves (Q-sort data) but not in the way they reacted to life experiences (PSI data).

Upon inspecting the data in depth, several other observations became apparent. First, the idea that the control group improved seems to be in question because that movement was not substantiated by parallel movement for the PSI. Second, idiographic analysis of the data revealed that the pooling of data for group treatment concealed considerable variability for individual subjects from the inception to the termination of therapy. That is, RS-IS correlations reveal that six subjects from the control group made gradual gains and that three made dramatic gains from the pretherapy (P_t) Period to the Time-One period (T_1) and then to the Time-Two period (T_2) (Table XVI).

Then, too, the absence of E_2 group movement seemed the result of isolated cases of regression. While some of the E_2 group

Figure 26

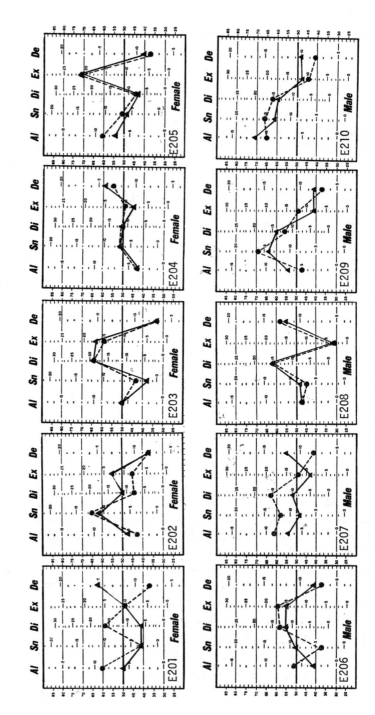

PSI PROFILE CHANGES FOR E_2 SUBJECTS
Credit Richard Lanyon, Author PSI.

TABLE XIV

SUMMARY OF MOVEMENT
INDICATIONS FOR OTHER-REFERRED (E_2) SUBJECTS

Subjects	Q-Sort RS - IS Relationships				PSI Factors										Emotional Stress Checklist	
					Al		Sn		Di		Ex		De			
	ISC	T_1	T_2	K	T_1	T_2	T_1	T_2	T_1	T_2	T_1	T_2	T_1	T_2	T_1	T_2
E201	.89	.40	.69	3.0	9	6	3	3	16	6	10	10	8	15	93	90
E202	.71	.56	.25	- 3.7	4	5	12	11	8	11	8	13	8	8	88	108
E203	.89	.45	.75	3.0	6	6	4	2	19	19	15	17	7	7	76	94
E204	.81	.32	.51	2.3	4	4	7	7	11	11	10	8	13	14	59	57
E205	.74	.46	.55	1.0	9	7	7	6	8	7	21	21	8	9	69	98
E206	.70	.45	.52	.8	6	3	4	9	13	12	17	15	7	8	97	62
E207	.74	-.29	.19	11.0	9	7	12	8	16	10	12	9	8	12	92	19
E208	.94	.70	.79	.9	5	5	7	8	15	15	3	3	13	12	42	52
E209	.72	.35	.24	- 1.8	5	7	16	14	12	14	12	8	7	8	143	91
E210	.78	.42	.69	2.6	10	12	15	13	15	14	10	11	8	10	80	105

members benefited from therapy, idiographic analysis revealed that two of the subjects regressed so seriously that they countered any real gains by the remaining seven.

From such observations, it now appears that a more reasonable approach to research may be to consider data exclusively in terms of idiographic movement. This would eliminate the restrictions imposed by averaging the performance of subjects who made considerable gains, those who remained constant, and those who regressed.

Finally, it is apparent from this research that people can experience attitudinal change and that, when they do, they feel more positive about themselves and reflect this new positivism in their respective relationships with others. It is also apparent that therapists and others who are employed in helping relationships can be trained to bring about such positive changes and can, in fact, when others seek help, implement a relationship which is both operationally definitive and functionally effective. In a sense, the approach we have used in establishing and maintaining professional relationships is keyed by the concept of accountability and nurtured by the results of the research which supports it.

Figure 27

T_1 ●———●

T_2 ▲———▲

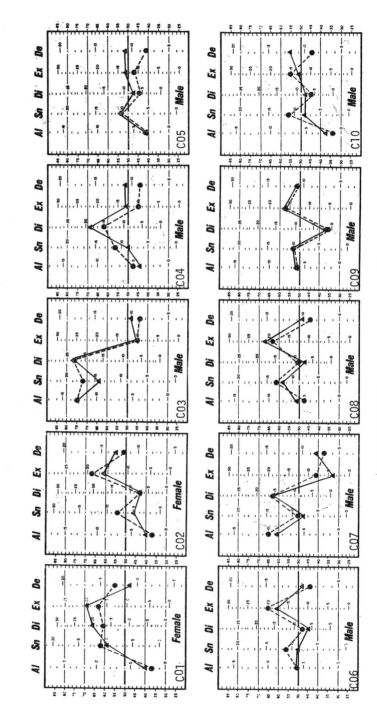

PSI PROFILE CHANGES FOR CONTROL SUBJECTS

TABLE XV

SUMMARY OF MOVEMENT
INDICATIONS FOR CONTROL (C) SUBJECTS

Subjects	Q-Sort RS - IS Relationships				PSI Factors									
					Al		Sn		Di		Ex		De	
	ISC	T_1	T_2	K	T_1	T_2	T_1	T_2	T_1	T_2	T_1	T_2	T_1	T_2
C01	.92	.77	.84	.5	2	3	11	10	4	4	17	20	13	11
C02	.75	.67	.71	.3	2	3	8	5	7	7	19	16	12	13
C03	.70	-.25	-.42	- 2.3	13	13	17	14	23	23	10	10	9	10
C04	.76	.41	.67	2.5	5	4	11	9	15	19	10	13	9	11
C05	.85	.83	.91	.7	3	3	10	10	6	7	11	13	8	11
C06	.81	.54	.79	2.0	6	6	11	9	8	6	20	18	9	10
C07	.79	.09	.21	2.5	10	9	9	8	16	16	8	4	7	8
C08	.82	.69	.73	.3	5	6	13	12	9	7	19	21	9	10
C09	.80	.73	.90	1.3	6	6	10	10	1	2	16	16	11	11
C10	.82	.41	.60	2.0	1	2	11	8	6	7	15	13	9	12

TABLE XVI

IS-RS RELATIONSHIP (PEARSON r'S) FOR ALL GROUPS
AT MATCHED TIME PERIODS

E_1 Group (N = 10)		E_2 Group (N = 10)			C Group (N = 10)		
T_1	T_2	P_c	T_1	T_2	P_t	T_1	T_2
.39	.80	.04	.40	.69	.66	.77	.84
—.25	.67	.47	.56	.25	.30	.67	.71
.13	.33	.33	.45	.75	.06	—.25	—.42
.36	.54	—.06	.32	.51	.52	.41	.67
—.25	.74	.67	.46	.55	.73	.83	.91
—.34	.46	.47	.45	.52	.51	.54	.79
.32	.85	—.33	—.29	.19	.22	.09	.21
.49	.61	.50	.70	.79	.22	.69	.73
—.20	.28	.08	.35	.24	.74	.73	.90
—.30	.67	.27	.42	.69	.15	.41	.60

BIBLIOGRAPHY

Allport, G.W. The functional autonomy of motives. *American Journal of Psychology*, 1937, ... 141-156.

Arbuckle, D.S. In W. Van Hoose & J. Pietrofiesa (Eds.), *Counseling and guidance in the twentieth century*. Boston: Houghton Mifflin, 1970.

Ausubel, D. *Theory and problems of child development*. New York: Grune & Stratton, 1957.

Baer, D.M. A technique of social reinforcement for the study of child behavior. Behavior avoiding reinforcement withdrawal. *Child Development*, 1962, *33*, 847-858.

Bandura, A. *Principles of behavior modification*. New York: Holt, Reinhart & Winston, 1969.

Bandura, A. *Relationship of family patterns to child behavior disorders*. Report, V.S.P.H. Research Grant M-1734, Stanford University, 1960.

Bandura, A., and Walters, R.H. *Adolescent aggression*. New York: Ronald, 1959.

Bandura, A., & Walters, R.H. Social learning of dependence behavior. In Million, *Theories of psychopathology*. Philadelphia: W.B. Saunders, 1967.

Bayles, E.E. *Democratic educational theory*. New York: Harper & Row, 1960.

Beach, F.A., Hebb, D.O., Morgan, C.T., & Nissen, H. *The neuro-psychology of Lashley*. New York: McGraw-Hill, 1960.

Berne, E. *What do you say after you say hello?* New York: Grove Press, 1972.

Bigge, M.L. *Learning theory for teachers*. New York: Harper & Row, 1964.

Bijou, S., Peterson, R.F., & Ault, M.H. A method to investigate descriptive and experimental field studies at the level of data and empirical concepts. *Journal of Applied Behavior Analysis*, 1968, *1*, 175-191.

Bixler, R.H. The changing world of the counselor: I. New approaches needed. *Counselor Education and Supervision, II* 1963, *4*, 100-105.

Bond, M. *The effect of first impression information upon behavior emitted during subsequent interaction*. Unpublished doctoral dissertation, Stanford University, 1970.

Boss, M. *Psychoanalysis and daseinanalysis*. New York: Basic Books, 1963.

Buytendijk, F.J.J. The phenomenological approach to the problems of feelings and emotions. In M.L. Reymest (Ed.), *Feelings and emotions*. New York: McGraw-Hill, 1950.

Cairns, R.B. *Antecedents of social reinforcer effectiveness*. Unpublished manuscript. Indiana University, 1962.

172

Callis, R. Toward an integrated theory of counseling. In B. Ard (Ed.), *Counseling and psychotherapy I.* Palo Alto, CA: Service and Behavior Books, 1966.

Callis, R. Toward in integrated theory of counseling. In B. Ard (Ed.), *Counseling and psychotherapy II.* Palo Alto, CA: Service and Behavior Books, 1966.

Cartwright, R.D., & Vogel, J.S. A comparison of changes in psychoneurotic patients during matched periods of therapy and no therapy. *Journal of Consulting Psychology,* 1960, *XXIV,* 121-217.

Chomsky, N. Review of B.F. Skinner, Verbal Behavior. *Language, 1959, 35,* 26-58.

Corsini, R.I. *Manual of instruction of the Chicago Q-sort.* Chicago: Chicago Psychological Affiliates, 1959.

Crites, J.O. Career counseling: a review of major approaches. *The Counseling Psychologist,* 1974, *4(3),* 11.

DiLoreto, A. *Comparative psychotherapy.* New York: Aldine-Aatherton, 1971.

Ellis, A. Goals of psychotherapy. In A. Mahrer (Ed.), *The goals of psychotherapy.* New York: Appleton-Century-Crofts, 1967.

Eysenck, H.J. The effects of psychotherapy: an evaluation. *Journal of Counseling Psychology,* 1952, *XVI,* 322.

Eysenck, H.J. Learning theory and behavior therapy. *Journal of Mental Science,* 1959, *105,* 61-75.

Eysenck, H.J. The outcome problem in psychotherapy: a reply. *Psychotherapy: Theory, Research, and Practice,* 1964, *I,* 97-100.

Eysenck, H.J. *The Effects of Psychotherapy, II.* New York: The International Science Press, 1966.

Festinger, L.A. *A theory of cognitive dissonance.* New York: Harper & Row, 1957.

Ford, D.H., & Urban, H.B. *Systems of psychotherapy.* New York: John Wiley and Sons, 1964.

Freud, S. Beyond the pleasure principle (1919). In J. Strachey (Ed.), *Standard Edition* (Vol. 18). London: Hogarth Press, 1955.

Goble, F. *The third force.* New York: Pocket Books, 1970.

Grebstein, L.C. *Toward self-understanding.* Glenview, IL, Scott, Foresman and Co., 1969.

Gutsch, K.U., & Mueller, R.K. Measuring counseling effectiveness through innovative research. *The Southern Journal of Educational Research,* 1975, *9,* 1-37.

Gutsch, K.U., & Peters, H.J. *Counseling with youth: in search for identity.* Columbus: Charles E. Merrill, 1973.

Harper, R.H. *Psychoanalysis and psychotherapy.* Englewood Cliffs: Prentice-Hall, 1959.

Hartup, W.W. Nurturance and nurturance withdrawal in relation to dependency behavior of pre-school children. *Child Development,* 1958, *29,* 191-201.

Hill, W.F. *Learning: a survey of psychological interpretations.* San Francisco: Chandler, 1963.

Horney, K. *Self analysis.* New York: Norton, 1942.

Jones, S.C., & Panitch, D. The self-fulfilling prophecy and interpersonal attraction. *Journal of Experimental Social Psychology,* 1971, *1,* 356-366.

Kessler, J.W. *Psychopathology of childhood.* Englewood Cliffs: Prentice-Hall, 1966.

Kluckhohn, C., & Murray, H.A. Personality foundation: determinants. In C. Grebstein (Ed.), *Toward Self Understanding.* Glenview, IL, Scott, Foresman and Co., 1969.

Kretchevsky, I. The genesis of "hypotheses" in rats. *University of California Publications in Psychology,* 1932, *6,* 45-54.

Laing, R.D. *The divided self.* New York: Pantheon Press, 1969.

Lazarus, R.S. *Psychological stress and the coping process.* New York: McGraw-Hill, 1966.

Lazarus, R.S. Emotions and adaption: conceptual and empirical relations. In W.J. Arnold (Ed.), *Nebraska Symposium on Motivation* (Vol. 16). Lincoln: University of Nebraska Press, 1968.

Levitt, E.E. The results of psychotherapy with children: an evaluation. *Journal of Consulting Psychology,* 1957, *XXI,* 189-196.

Malan, D.H. The outcome problem in psychotherapy research. *Archives of General Psychiatry,* 1973, *29,* 719-729.

May, R. *Existential psychology.* New York: Random House, 1960.

May, R. *Existence.* New York: Simon & Schuster, 1967.

Mendels, J. *Concepts of depression.* New York: John Wiley & Sons, 1970.

Millon, T. *Theories of psychopathology.* Philadelphia: W.B. Saunders, 1967.

Mischel, W. On the future of personality measurement. *American Psychologist,* 1977, *32,* 246-254.

Misiak, H., and Sexton, V. *Phenomenological, existential and humanistic psychologies — a historical survey.* New York: Grune & Stratton, 1973.

Milhollan, F., & Forisha, B. *From Skinner to Rogers.* Lincoln, NE, Professional Educators Publications, Inc., 1972.

Mowrer, O.H. Learning theory and the neurotic paradox. *American Journal of Orthopsychiatry,* 1948, *18,* 871-910.

Murphy, L. Coping devices and defense mechanisms in relation to autonomous ego functions. *The Bulletin of the Menninger Clinic,* 1960, *24,* 144-153.

Osipow, S.H. *Strategies in counseling for behavior change.* New York: Appleton-Century-Crofts, 1970.

Patterson, C.H. The irrelevancy of wishful thinking: part two. *Counselor Education and Supervision,* 1964, *IV*(1), 21-22.

Raimy, V. Phrenophobia and disabling anxiety. In A.R. Mahrer (Ed.),

The Goals of psychotherapy. New York: Appleton-Century-Crofts, 1967.

Ritchie, B.F., Aeschliman, B. & Peirce, P. Studies in spatial learning. *Journal of Comparative and Physiological Psychology*, 1950, *43*:73-85.

Rogers, C.R. A theory of therapy, personality, and interpersonal relationships as developed in the client-centered framework. In S. Koch (Ed.), *Psychology: A study of science.* McGraw-Hill, 1959.

Rogers, C.R. *Client-centered therapy.* Boston: Houghton-Mifflin, 1951.

Rogers, C.R. *On becoming a person.* Boston: Houghton-Mifflin, 1961.

Rogers, C. A theory of personality. In T. Millon (Ed.), *Theories of Psychopathology.* Philadelphia: W.B. Saunders, 1967.

Ruch, F.L., & Zimbardo, P.G. *Psychology and Life* (8th ed.). Glenview, IL: Scott, Foresman, & Co., 1971.

Sartre, J.P. *Existential Psychoanalysis.* New York: Philosophical Library, 1953.

Sax, G. *Empirical Foundations of educational research.* Englewood Cliffs: Prentice-Hall, 1968.

Schoon, C.G., & Strahmann, R.F. Use of the psychological screening inventory in a university service. *Journal of Counseling Psychology*, 1971, *18*, 367-368.

Skinner, B.F. B.F. Skinner and radical behaviorism. In K. Dye, *Three Views of Man.* Belmont, CA: Wadsworth, 1975.

Skinner, B.F. What is psychotic behavior? In T. Millon (Ed.), *Theories of psychopathology.* Philadelphia: W.B. Saunders, 1967, 324-337.

Sloane, C.B., et al. *Psychotherapy vs. Behavior Therapy.* Cambridge, MA: Harvard University Press, 1975.

Stefflre, B. In W. Van Hoose & J. Pietrofiesa (Eds.), *Conseling and guidance in the twentieth century.* Boston: Houghton Mifflin, 1970.

Stephenson, W. *The study of behavior: Q-technique and its methodology.* Chicago: The University of Chicago Press, 1953.

Sullivan, H.S. *Concepts of modern psychiatry.* Washington, D.C.: William Alanson White Psychiatric Foundation, 1947.

Super, D.E. Career patterns as a basis for vocational counseling. *Journal of Counseling Psychology*, 1954, *1*, 12-20.

Tyler, L. The work of the counselor. In J. Huber & H. Millman (Eds.), *Goals and Behavior in psychotherapy.* Columbus: Charles E. Merrill, 1972.

Ullman, A.D. Time as a determinant in integrative learning. *Psychology Review*, 1945, *52*, 61-90.

Walker, T.M. *Introduction to Computer Science: An Interdisciplinary Approach.* Boston: Allyn and Bacon, 1972.

Wallis, W.A. and Roberts, H.V. *Statistics: a new approach.* New York: The Free Press of Glenco, 1956.

Wolpe, J. *Psychotherapy by reciprocal inhibition.* Stanford, CA: Stanford University Press, 1958.

Wolpe, J. *The practice of behavior therapy.* New York: Pergamon Press, 1969.

INDEX

A

Aeschliman, B., 9
Algorithmic schematization
  annotation box, 40
  decision box, 40
  definition of, 38, 39
  flowchart language, 39-42
  flowline, 41
  in-connector, 41
  off-page connector, 41
  out-connector, 41
  processing box, 40
  terminal box, 39
Allport, G., 5
Anxiety, 35
Ausubel, D., 19

B

Baer, D.M., 66
Bandura, A., 133
Beach, F.A., 9
Behaviorism and humanism, 10, 11, 19-22, 42
Berne, E., 81
Bigge, M.L., xi, 56
Bijou, S., 144
Bixler, R.H., 64
Boss, M., 123
Butendijk, F.J.J., 5

C

Cairns, R.B., 133
Callis, R., 67, 85
Cartwright, R.D., 64
Case of Denny, 112
  coping strategies, 112
  fear of the future, 113
  flowcharts of intervention therapy, 124, 128
  group experience, 115
  impact of the group, 126
  insights, 121
  masking, 127
  moving toward people, 129
  primary learning route, 118
  reality testing, 125
  rigidity as a coping strategy, 114
  search for identity, 116
  self-hate, 117
  sordid past, 115
Case of Mat, 65
  analyzing statements, 79, 89-93
  destiny, 67
  experiences leading to depression, 70, 71
  flowchart learning route, 73
  flowchart problem intervention, 92
  flowchart therapeutic intervention, 80
  life style, 72
  mother, 70
  pattern formation, 108
  philosophy of life, 72
  press technique, 76
  road to depression, 71
  schematic interpretation, 108
  search for identity, 68
  theoretical persuasion, 85-86
  transcript segments, 101-109
Case of Paul, 129
  desperation, 129
  dramatic bent, 130
  flowchart, 134
  search for identity, 131
Chomsky, N., 9
Closure
  definition of, 5, 15, 16, 46
Compulsivity, 30
Computed Units of Emotional Stress (CUES), 29, 30
Confrontation
  definition of, 34
Coping strategies, 25

case of Denny, 112
definition of, 4, 7, 35
dual consequences, 7, 35, 45
illustrated, 4
rigidity as, 114
three basic moves, 26
Corsini, Q-Sort, 138-165
Counter conditioning
definition of, 34, 35

D

Desensitization
definition of, 34
Diloreto, A., 64
Dispirited Syndrome, 26
algorithmic schematization, 46
Dramatic Syndrome, 28
algorithmic schematization, 46

E

Ellis, A., 11
Emotional Stress Checklist (ESC), 60, 147
Eysenck, H.J., 5, 19, 64, 86

F

Festinger, L.A., 36
Figure 1: Learning process, 43
Figure 2: Changing attitudes, 48
Figure 3: Environmental Blocks, 55
Figure 4: Faulty method of operation, 58
Figure 5: Mat's primary learning route, 73
Figure 6: Type I, problem intervention, 80
Figure 7: Type I, problem intervention, 92
Figure 8: Type II, problem intervention, 97
Figure 9: Type II, problem intervention, 109
Figure 10: Type II, problem intervention, 110
Figure 11: Denny's primary learning route, 118
Figure 12: Type I, problem intervention, 124
Figure 13: Type II, problem intervention, 128

Figure 14: Paul's primary learning route, 134
Figure 15: Emotional Stress Checklist (ESC), 147
Figure 16-20: Plotting self actualizing tendencies, 151-157
Figures 21, 22, 23, 24: Q-Sort movement, 159-162
Figures 25, 26, 27: PSI profile changes, 166, 168, 170
Ford, D.H., 64
Freud, S., 65

G

Goble, F., 5
Grebstein, L.C., 9, 35
Gutsch, K.U., 18, 20, 142, 146

H

Hartup, W.W., 66
Hebb, D.O., 9
Hill, W.F., 42
Horney, K., 26, 108, 112
Humanism and behaviorism, 10, 11, 19-22, 42

I

Identity
behavior change, 15, 87
Denny's search for identity, 16
Mat's search for identity, 68
Paul's search for identity, 131
risk as a means to personal identity, 83
searching for personal identity, 16, 24
Impulsivity, 30

J

Juxtaposition
definition of, 8
illustrated, 31, 32
psychoanalysis, in, 76

K

Kluckhohn, C., 19
Kretchevsky, I., 9

L

Laing, R.D., 25
Lazarus, R.S., 126

Learning
definition of, 15, 42, 89
implications for, 42-46
Levitt, E.E., 64

M

Malan, D.H., 64
Man
dependent variable, 5
independent variable, 5
nature, 10
search for identity, 15
May, R., 5, 10, 12
Mendels, J., 84
Metalanguage
definition of, 12
illustrated, 12
key to understanding, 81
part of the syndromes, 26
Mihollan, F., and Forisha, B., 3, 10
Millon, T., 17
Mischel, W., 9
Misiak, H., 99
Modeling, 22, 24, 50
Morgan, C.T., 9
Mowrer, O.H., 16
Mueller, R.K., 20
Murray, H.A., 19

N

Nexus psychotherapy
analysis through algorithm, 38
art of, 64
definition of, 3
differs from other therapies, 5, 7
essential steps to therapy, 8
how implemented, 6, 21, 22
how learning takes place, 18, 19
human aspects, 18
Nexus therapist in action, 98
operational procedures, 21, 22
potential stress, 4
problem intervention, 50
reality split, 4
research, 136-171
role of therapist, 36, 89
science of, 84
theory, 16, 17
two step approach to therapy, 7

Type I problem defined, 7, 20, 47-55
Type II problem defined, 7, 20, 56-63
working with client
Computed Units of Emotional Stress (CUES), 29, 30
examining coping strategies, 25
learned controls, 23
listening, 22
modeling, 22
reality testing, 32
relaxation as a key concept, 24, 25
risking, 23
studying patterns of reaction, 25
viewing incongruencies tactfully, 23
Nissen, H., 9

O

Osipow, S.H., 10

P

Pattern formation
definition of, 8, 9, 22, 25
Mat's patterns, 79
Patterson, C.H., 64
Perception
faulty, definition of, 7, 8
incongruencies, 20, 21
perception *vs.* reality, 4, 43
Perceptual chipping
definition of, 8
illustrated, 31
Peters, H., 18, 146
Philosophy, 10, 89
Pierce, P., 9
Press technique
implementing (the press), 31, 52
juxtaposition, 8, 31, 32, 51
perceptual chipping, 8, 31, 51
recapitulation, 8, 32, 52
with Mat, 76
Psychotherapy
art of, 14, 15, 84
definition of, 14, 15
role of the therapist, 36
science of, 14, 15, 84

R

Reality
bridging the gap, 52, 53

perception, *vs.*, 4, 43
results of reality testing, 53, 54
testing attitudinal changes, 22, 32, 45
Research
  Emotional Stress Checklist (ESC), 138,
    143, 161
  ESC movement and Q-Sort results, 150
  need for, 136
  plotting self actualizing tendencies,
    150, 151
  Psychological Screening Inventory,
    (PSI), 138
  results of the study
    ESC results, Table XI
    Figures 21-24, 159-162
    PSI results, Figures 25-27, 166-170
    Q-Sort results, 159-162
  speculation about research, 138
  testing new ideas, 141
Rigid Syndrome, 26, 27
  algorithmic schematization, 46
Risk
  consequences, 8
  definition of, 20, 23
  key to change, 75
  reality testing, 53
Ritchie, B.F., 9
Roberts, H.V., 157
Rogers, C., 3, 4, 5, 10, 64

S

Sartre, J.P., 6, 9
Sax, G., 144
Schoon, C.G., 141
Sexton, V., 99
Skinner, B.F., 5, 9
Sloane, C.B., 64
Stahmann, R.F., 141
Stefflre, B., 14
Stephenson, W., 142
Stress, defintion of, 4
Sullivan, H.S., 14
Super, D.G., 6, 11, 17, 18
Synergy, 6

T

Tables
  Table I: Nexus therapy with dispir-
    ited clients, 59
  Table II: Nexus therapy with rigid
    clients, 59
  Table III: Nexus therapy with dra-
    matic clients, 60
  Table IV: Client ratings, 142
  Table V: Rating of tapes, 144
  Table VI: Coefficients of interrater
    agreement for rating of tapes, 145
  Table VII: Consistency of rating of
    tapes overtime, 145
  Table VIII: Coefficients of intra-
    rater stability, 145
  Table IX: Ideal self constants for
    Q-Sorts, 157
  Table X: *Z* score means for *self* re-
    ferred clients, 164
  Table XI: ESC ratings for two ex-
    perimental groups, 164
  Table XII: PSI statistics for self re-
    ferred clients, 164
  Table XIII: Summary of movements
    for self referred subjects, 167
  Table XIV: Summary of movements
    for other referred subjects, 169
  Table XV: Summary of movements
    for control subjects, 171
  Table XVI: IS-RS relationship for
    all groups researched, 171
Therapist's role
  agent of change, 36
  Mat's case, 89
Tyler, L., 82

U

Ullman, A.D., 16
Urban, H.B., 64

W

Walker, T.M., 38
Wallis, W.A., 157
Walters, R.H., 133
Wolpe, J., 5, 12